WHAT YOU NEED TO KNOW ABOUT NEWBORNS &
BREASTFEEDING IN AN EASY-TO-READ SURVIVAL GUIDE

NEWBORN CARE & BREASTFEEDING BIBLE

FROM A CERTIFIED BREASTFEEDING SPECIALIST &
INTERNATIONAL BOARD CERTIFIED LACTATION CONSULTANT

Miranda Farmer RN, BSN, CBS, IBCLC

Newborn Care & Breastfeeding Bible

Copyright © 2023 Miranda Farmer

All rights reserved.

Medical Disclaimer: The information provided in this book is intended solely for general educational and informational purposes only. It is neither intended nor implied to be a substitute for professional medical advice. Always seek the advice of your healthcare provider for any questions you may have regarding your or your infant's medical condition. Never disregard professional medical advice or delay in seeking it because of something you have received in this book. The author has provided general information and cannot make any assurances in regard to the applicability of any information to any particular person in any particular set of circumstances. The reader assumes all risk of taking any action or making any decision based on the information contained in this book. The author shall have no liability or responsibility for any such action taken or decision made by any reader of this book, and no liability for any loss, injury, damage, or impairment allegedly arising from the information provided in this book.

ISBN: 9798866054213 (Paperback)
ISBN: 9798871067178 (Hardcover)

Front cover image by photographer Sarah Bracci
Edited By Richard Davis

First printing, 2023

www.ThePostpartumNurse.org

Special thanks to my husband, Bradley, for supporting my crazy aspirations while I wrote this book on maternity leave with our first son.

Author
MIRANDA FARMER
RN, BSN, CBS, IBCLC

I am a Postpartum (AKA Mother-Baby) Nurse, Lactation Consultant, and mother currently working both in the hospital and independent setting. I work with new parents on a daily basis, teaching the basics of newborn care and breastfeeding. My credentials include RN (Registered Nurse), BSN (Bachelor of Science in Nursing), CBS (Certified Breastfeeding Specialist), and IBCLC (International Board-Certified Lactation Consultant).

I make free TikTok videos teaching new moms how to breastfeed and care for their newborn. To view my videos, search @ThePostpartumNurse on TikTok.

TikTok @ThePostpartumNurse

Instagram @ThePostpartumNurse

www.ThePostpartumNurse.org

LACTATION CONSULTANT

TABLE OF CONTENTS

Why Read This Book?	1
How to Use this Book	3
Decisions During Pregnancy	4
Making Informed Decisions	9
The Golden Hours	10
Umbilical Cord Clamping	12
Kangaroo Care	13
Newborn Transition	15
Newborn Medications	17
The Third Stage of Labor – The Placenta	19
The First Latch	21
What to Expect from Your Newborn	23
Postpartum Hospital Stay	25
Newborn Testing	27
Safe Sleep	30
SIDS	33
Benefits of Breastfeeding	35
Colostrum	39
Hand Expression	41
Antenatal Colostrum Harvesting	43

Breastmilk Storage	45
Breastmilk Composition	47
Breastfeeding & Latching	53
Signs of a Good vs Poor Feeding	61
Breastfeeding Positions	63
Feeding on Demand	66
Milk Supply	68
Perceived Low Supply	72
Cluster Feeding	74
Average Milk Volume	76
Poops/Pees (Output)	78
Newborn Weight Gain	81
Newborn Sleep Cycles	84
When Do You Get to Sleep?	86
Second Night Syndrome	87
Waking a Sleepy Baby	90
Latching Problems & Damaged Nipples	92
Formula AKA Human Milk Replacement	102
Pumping	107
Clogged Ducts and Mastitis	111
Jaundice	115
Umbilical Cord and Bathing	117
Diapering Tips	119

Postpartum Depression/Baby Blues	121
Summary: Survival in the first 2 weeks	124
Gems from Experienced Moms	127
How Can Your Support Person Help	129
When to Call a Lactation Consultant	130
To the Reader	131
References	134

WHY READ THIS BOOK?

As a Postpartum Nurse, most new parents I work with have never seen a baby breastfeed, have never taken a breastfeeding class, and some have never held a newborn. You can imagine, it is very difficult to learn everything there is to know about newborns in one to two days in a hospital while you're sleep deprived. I could write a 300-page book on everything you could know about newborns; it is impossible to learn all of this in the immediate postpartum period. However, this is the reality and expectation of most parents.

Breastfeeding, though natural, is a learned skill and takes practice. You should utilize this book to learn how to breastfeed and care for your newborn before you deliver. This book will set you up for success.

I don't know where we went wrong as a society in the US. Maybe it was when we started living in more separate households the skill of breastfeeding and newborn care was lost. Women were no longer learning from other women when they gave birth and caring for their newborns. In society today, we are taught to cover ourselves when breastfeeding to protect decency, but at what cost?

We, as a culture, are no longer observing these first few moments between mom and baby, nor are we seeing newborns breastfeed. The skill is lost between generations and within communities because we are so divided. You can relate this phenomenon to animals in a zoo who are raised in captivity. One example is a gorilla who was born and raised in an Ohio zoo. She had never seen a baby gorilla nurse, so when she gave birth to her own baby, she did not know what to do. She had no concept of breastfeeding, and the baby sadly died. When she became pregnant again, the La Leche League and volunteer breastfeeding moms went to the zoo and breastfed their infants in front of the pregnant gorilla. When the baby was born, the volunteers were there to show her what to do and the gorilla was able to breastfeed by mimicking the nursing mothers' movements. We, as a culture, lack this observation and teaching between moms, but we can get it back.

This book will walk you through the newborn process in a way other books don't because it is written by a postpartum nurse and lactation consultant. I get these questions every day and I know what the most common concerns are. We will explore these together so you will feel prepared going into the journey of parenthood and breastfeeding.

HOW TO USE THIS BOOK

It is best to read this book in the last trimester of pregnancy so you can be best prepared before you deliver your baby, and the information is still fresh in your mind. It may seem silly but practice the breastfeeding techniques presented in this book often using a stuffed animal or baby doll. Then, once your baby us here, utilize this book as a reference throughout your breastfeeding journey.

This book is intended to be interactive, with scannable QR codes throughout, linking you to evidence-based research articles and practices. To visit the websites within the QR codes, simply scan the code with your phone camera. The websites are also listed in the "Links" section of this book.

Congratulations and welcome to parenthood!

DECISIONS DURING PREGNANCY

Throughout pregnancy and the birth process, there are many decisions you will need to make on behalf of you and your baby. It is important to know what medical interventions you are agreeing to and make informed decisions. Many "routine" medical interventions are created to benefit the masses rather than the individual and they may not always be in your best interest. This book will cover many topics and give evidence-based information, but it is still up to you to make informed decisions that are best for you and your family.

Research and discuss the following with your partner (BEFORE delivery) to make an informed decision **for your baby:**

- Vitamin K injection and Erythromycin eye ointment (given after birth, routinely)
- Circumcision (elective, sometimes in the hospital, sometimes outpatient)
- Who will your pediatrician be? (usually need to know by 24 hours old for Newborn Screen documents)
- Hepatitis B Vaccine (routinely at 24 hours old)
- Bath in the hospital (not recommended in hospital anymore – better for breastfeeding, wait *at least* 24 hours)

- Rooming-in (baby should be kept in your room with you, not the nursery, if medically possible)
- Breastfeeding vs. formula feeding (pros and cons to each)
- Hand expression before delivery (AKA Antenatal colostrum harvesting)
- Safe sleep guidelines (will you use a crib, bassinette, bedside sleeper, etc.)

It is a good idea to know what the "routine interventions" are at the hospital/birth center you are delivering at and to **know your preferences** before you go in to deliver.

Also, know what your healthcare provider's thoughts are on the following routine medical interventions in labor and delivery such as:

- Mandatory peripheral IV
- IV fluids throughout labor
- Epidural vs alternative pain control methods
- Routine IV Pitocin in 3rd stage of labor (after baby is born to prevent bleeding)
- Episiotomies
- Vacuum extraction
- Coached pushing vs laboring down
- Continuous fetal monitoring

Most of these interventions listed above for the laboring mother are not beneficial and can lead to additional complications and medical interventions. Know ahead of time which you agree with and which you want to decline. Visit the link to the right for  more information on these practices. Just make sure your health care provider (HCP) and their medical group agrees with your decisions or if certain interventions are mandatory. Remember, you can ALWAYS switch providers, no matter where you are in pregnancy, if they do not align with your beliefs or wishes.

Remember, your HCP may not actually even be the one who delivers your baby, most likely it will be whoever is "on-call" from their group. Ask your HCP about how this works for their specific practice. Also, the HCP is generally only there for the end of the pushing stage and delivery of the placenta; the nurses are the ones who are there for the entire labor and delivery process. Many people are surprised to discover this when they have their first baby! The doctor or HCP is only there for what feels like 5 minutes. I highly suggest reading this eBook for more information on these topics. For more information about having a healthy birth, access the Lamaze eBook from the QR code here:

PRENATAL CLASSES: It is a great idea to take a Prenatal Breastfeeding course **BEFORE** you deliver. I am a huge proponent of this in the last few weeks of pregnancy because it is much easier to learn and absorb information when you are not sleep deprived. Do not expect to learn everything about breastfeeding in the hospital, the nurses will be busy with other things, most of the time. It is usually best to take a prenatal breastfeeding education course in the last trimester of pregnancy, so the information is fresh in your mind, but you also have time to practice the techniques of breastfeeding. Breastfeeding is natural, but it doesn't always come easy.

Also, taking a childbirth education course and reading books *with* your support person is definitely a good idea to prepare you for the birth process. This book will prepare you for the newborn phase and how to survive (and thrive) with your newborn; however, this book does *not* prepare you for labor or delivery.

There are many techniques for coping through labor, I would suggest starting with the link to Lamaze healthy birth practices above and going from there. If you are planning for an unmedicated birth, many practices and techniques exist for natural coping strategies such as Hypnobirthing, Bradley method, Spinning Babies, Lamaze, utilizing a Doula, Water Birth, Hydrotherapy, etc. Most of these practices are centered around staying upright for labor and having the ability to move, continuous labor support, breathing techniques, creating a soothing environment and physical/mental relaxation. If you are choosing to do an epidural or utilize IV pain medications, please research the "cascade of interventions" and be sure you are making informed decisions about your care. It is **ALWAYS** ok to ask questions.

MAKING INFORMED DECISIONS:

A good acronym to remember for making an informed decision for any medical intervention is **BRAIN**:

Benefits

Risks

Alternatives

Intuition (what does your intuition say)

Now or **N**ever? (What if you don't do the intervention at this moment and what if you never do it?)

Remember to ask these things when your medical provider/nurse suggests a routine or medical intervention to be sure you are making informed decisions for you and your baby.

THE GOLDEN HOURS

In some hospitals in the US, when your baby is born, the nurses will immediately take your baby away from you to a warmer to dry them, weigh them, and measure them. This immediate separation is very stressful to the newborn and does not support their transition into life outside of your body nor does it support breastfeeding.

If we go back to basics and think of the birth process in other animals, it is extremely important for the mother and baby to have immediate and uninterrupted contact. Separation can be detrimental to the mother-baby dyad in most animals. And, after all, humans are still part of the animal kingdom.

Keeping your baby skin-to-skin with you in these first few hours decreases both of your stress hormones, stabilizes their breathing and heart rate, maintains their temperature and blood sugar levels, increases your milk production, and increases attachment. Your body is the perfect design as their habitat and warms them to the ideal body temperature. Think of your body as your baby's entire ecosystem; you are the best thing for them to create physiologic stability.

We call these first 1-2 hours after delivery the "Golden Hours," AKA the sacred hours because of how important they are for a baby's transition into the world and a mother's transition into motherhood. During this time, all non-essential medical interventions for your baby can wait (like weighing them, measuring, etc.) and your baby should be kept skin-to-skin with you against your body. Hospitals and birth centers labeled as "Baby Friendly" will automatically create an environment for this undisturbed golden hour, but if your hospital does not have the Baby Friendly designation, you can still discuss the golden hour with your care team ahead of time and advocate for it.

UMBILICAL CORD CLAMPING

In most hospitals, umbilical cord clamping will generally be "delayed" for 30-60 seconds routinely, but the current recommendation is to **wait to clamp until the cord stops pulsing or at least 2-3 minutes**. This is because, for the first few minutes after birth, there is still circulation from the placenta to the infant providing oxygen and nutrients.

This circulation of blood from the placenta and into your baby is called "placental transfusion." The majority of the transfusion occurs within 3 minutes after birth and provides iron reserves for your baby's first 6–8 months of life. This storage of iron prevents and delays iron deficiency in your baby until iron-fortified foods can be started.

Read more about the research here:

KANGAROO CARE

Wearing your baby "skin-to-skin" or in "kangaroo care" means your chest is completely exposed (no clothes), and baby is completely naked (except a diaper). When you are wearing your baby while in bed, make sure they are always in a vertical position on their tummy, right between your breasts. You should be semi-reclined to where you can comfortably rest, but not completely flat.

Also, you should always be able to see their face/mouth/nose to prevent suffocation. Skin-to-skin is also known as Kangaroo care because when you place a blanket over baby's back and under your body, you wear your baby in a pouch like a kangaroo. This position is very beneficial for bonding, breastfeeding, and your baby's transition into extra-uterine life.

Remember, wearing your baby skin-to-skin helps to maintain your baby's blood sugar levels (even without feeding them) and stabilizes your baby's heart rate, respiratory rate, temperature, and stress levels. Also, because baby is close to your breasts, it's easy to respond to baby's early hunger cues and gently guide baby onto the breast at your baby's pace. To read a full article about Kangaroo care, visit the link to the right.

You'll want to wear your baby skin-to-skin as much as possible, especially in the first few hours/days/months of life.

To make sure you are in a safe position, when your baby is on your chest, use pillows to support both of your arms and tuck a blanket behind baby 's back and under your sides to secure your baby to you. This will ensure you do not drop your baby if you accidentally fall asleep. There is a product called a Joey Pouch which is essentially a long, stretchy fabric strap with Velcro used for exactly this purpose; some hospitals give them to patients to use to promote baby wearing.

Skin-to-skin/baby wearing/kangaroo care should not end when you leave the hospital, it really should be just the beginning.

Once you get home, the more you "wear" your baby in a wrap and close to your body, the more comfortable you and your baby will be. Baby wearing helps to soothe your infant and it is easier to feed on demand when your infant is always close to you while you are also hands free.

NEWBORN TRANSITION

When your baby is first born, the nurses will generally check your and baby's vital signs (heart rate, respiratory rate, temp, blood pressure) every 30 minutes for the first two hours of life. This can be disruptive to the Golden Hours, but is important for your safety. These vital sign checks CAN BE completed with baby still skin-to-skin with you, so advocate to keep your baby on you!

If your baby needs any resuscitation or support with the transition into extra-uterine life, your nurses may take baby to an infant warmer in your room. Some babies don't get skin-to-skin time immediately, especially if they need to go to the NICU for closer observation. Your baby's body must make a lot of transitions when they go from living inside your uterus to outside in air and sometimes babies take longer to make those transitions.

One huge transition a baby must make is breathing on their own! Your baby's blood circulation when they are inside of you changes drastically when they take their first breath of air. As a fetus, your baby's blood  bypassed their lungs because they were getting oxygen from you via the placenta. Once they take their first breath, blood starts circulating into the lungs to carry oxygen to the rest of their body the same way we do as adults. If you want to learn more about fetal circulation, check out this article:

NEWBORN MEDICATIONS

Usually in the first two hours after delivery, your nurse will administer Vitamin K and Erythromycin eye ointment to your baby. The Vitamin K is an injection into your baby's thigh muscle and helps your baby to form clotting factors which are important for the prevention of bleeding and prevent rare but serious brain bleeds. Learn more by scanning the QR code shown to the right.

Erythromycin is an eye ointment that goes into your babies' eyes and prevents eye infection from "potential STD's" which *could* be present in mom's birth canal. Read more about it by scanning the QR code shown to the right. If you decide to have these medications administered to your baby, both may be given while baby is still skin-to-skin.

Some hospitals also give the Hepatitis B vaccine routinely within these first 2 hours of life, whereas others wait until the first 24 hours. This vaccine is the first of a series that protects against the Hepatitis B virus. This virus is spread through blood, semen, and other bodily fluids of an infected person. In 2020, only 2,157 total cases were reported to the CDC in the US whereas approximately 296 million people are affected worldwide.

THE THIRD STAGE OF LABOR – THE PLACENTA

After delivery of your baby, the placenta will detach from the wall of your uterus, and you will deliver that as well. The nurses will push on your tummy firmly to massage the top of your uterus (also called the fundus) to make sure it stays firm and contracts. Over the next six weeks, the uterus contracts to shrink down to pre-pregnancy size. During this time, you will continue to have vaginal bleeding as the spot on your uterus heals where the placenta detached. Think of that spot as a large scab. The placenta was a whole organ (an organ you GREW) that attached to your uterine wall with tiny blood vessels, which was very vascular (lots of blood flowing) to transport oxygen and nutrients between you and your baby during pregnancy.

Your vaginal bleeding will be present after delivery whether you had a C-section or vaginal birth, because of this! With a C-section, you might only see spotting for the few days after delivery, but it will generally be less than with a vaginal birth. By day 3 postpartum, your bleeding should be a pink/spotting flow. If you ever saturate more than 1 full large pad per hour, notify your doctor immediately. Also, if you pass any clots larger than the size of an egg or golf ball, notify your doctor. Stringy clots like you sometimes see with your period can be normal, but if you're seeing them frequently and your bleeding is increasing, notify your doctor. If you ever saturate one large pad in 30 minutes (2 pads per hour), notify your doctor immediately and go to the ER.

When you are breastfeeding after delivery (and up to 6 weeks after), you may feel contractions as your uterus clamps down or contracts. This is normal and, although it sucks, is imperative. I always say these contractions are, "pain with a purpose."

As you breastfeed your baby, your body secretes oxytocin (along with many other hormones), which cause the uterus to contract and prevents bleeding. Nipple stimulation after delivery has been shown to be as effective in preventing postpartum hemorrhages as synthetic oxytocin (the medication Pitocin they put into your IV).

If you are planning to breastfeed and not at a high risk for a postpartum hemorrhage, talk to your doctor beforehand about limiting the amount of Pitocin given to you during labor and after delivery. Some research has shown the more synthetic oxytocin received through labor and delivery, the less naturally occurring oxytocin your body produces, which can impact your milk supply.

After the delivery of the placenta, your doctor will check your vaginal opening and labia for any tears and repair them as needed. You can still wear your baby on your chest in the skin-to-skin position while they are doing these repairs, just ask.

THE FIRST LATCH

During the first hour of life, babies are usually more alert and will begin searching for your breasts. If allowed, babies will often self-attach to the breast in time. Mother responds to baby and gently assists baby to the nipple as a guide rather than a force, allowing the baby to lead the latch. This process, known as "the breast crawl," is infant-led feeding where babies can use their innate behaviors and instincts to literally crawl to the breast! If the baby is separated during this time, they are robbed of this biological process, which is another main reason why the golden hours should be uninterrupted from routine interventions.

Feeding your infant within the first hour of life is very important not only for them, but also for establishing your milk supply. By removing milk within the first hour, it sends signals to your body to make more milk when those signals are the strongest. This video by Jane Morton about these *First Droplets* is one of the most thorough videos about latching, hand expression, and establishing your milk supply early on.

If you are unable to latch your baby within this first hour for any reason, it is important to take your milk supply into your own hands and hand express to empty

the milk. By emptying this first milk, you send the strongest signals to your body to start establishing your milk supply.

WHAT TO EXPECT FROM YOUR NEWBORN

Your newborn will normally be delivered with their face pointing downward or backwards toward your rectum. If you hear your baby is "sunny side up" this is a variation of normal and their face will be facing upwards or in front of your body. It is important to prepare your support person for these delivery positions because it may be frightening when they see your baby crowning and the head deliver, but baby does not have a face (because it's pointing down).

Because of the compression from birth, the baby's head will usually be compressed/lengthened or "coned," but this cone shape will usually decrease in the next few hours-days. We call this "molding" as the baby's head was molded on the descent through your pelvis and it is perfectly normal. Make sure your support person knows this as well, as it can often be frightening to see.

APPEARANCE: Newborns will usually be a pinkish-blue or purple color when they are first born, but this should quickly transition to a pink or even red tone as their body begins to oxygenate via the lungs rather than the placenta. They may continue to have dark blue/purple hands and feet for the first 24-48 hours of life, this is called acrocyanosis and it basically means all their blood is going to the "important places" in their body such as the brain, lungs, heart, organs, etc.

Your baby may also be covered in a white, cheesy cream called Vernix Caseosa which coats their skin and is best to be rubbed in rather than washed off. At birth, your newborn will probably be wet from the amniotic fluid and blood that comes with delivery. Their face may look a bit smashed or creased, especially their nose, and their eyes may be puffy. The swelling will usually go down in the first few days.

BREATHING: Newborns will often have irregular, shallow breathing when they are first born. Their respiratory rate (how fast they are breathing) is usually faster than normal after delivery and within the first 2 hours after birth. This rate generally slows to a normal 30-60 breaths per minute or 1 breath per second maximum. They normally have irregular patterns of breathing, so they will breathe quickly then slow, so the respiratory rate is counted over a full minute to get the average breaths per minute.

This irregular breathing pattern is to be expected for newborns. Hiccups and sneezing are also normal and short periods of both are very common.

EYES: In the uterus, babies can see light and darkness. At birth, they usually can see the distance between their breastfeeding position and mother's face. Their vision slowly improves as they age, and further objects come into focus. Their eyes usually look like a dark blue/grey at birth, but the color slowly changes over the next few months.

POSTPARTUM HOSPITAL STAY

Generally, you will stay in the hospital for 24-48 hours for a vaginal delivery and 48-72 hours for a C-section, after the baby is born.

In some hospitals, you will stay in the labor & delivery room for the remainder of your hospital stay. In others, like mine, you will move to your Postpartum or Mother-Baby room and will get a new nurse. Some hospitals have nurses on 12-hour shifts, while others have 8-hour shifts or a combination of the two.

In some hospitals, the lactation consultant will see every patient, but others you will need a referral. Ask to see the lactation consultant, no matter what! It's never a bad idea to get more education or have a second set of eyes on your latch.

Before you leave the hospital, make sure you feel comfortable doing the following things:

- Changing your baby's diaper
- Bathing your baby (do not submerge until umbilical cord falls off)
- Dressing your baby
- Swaddling
- Feeding and burping your baby
- Breastfeeding positions
- Caring for a healing circumcision (if you elected for one)
- Using a bulb syringe

- Taking a newborn's temperature (under the armpit), what normal is
- Tips for soothing your baby
- Holding your newborn

ROOMING-IN: During your hospital stay, the baby should be kept in your room, AKA rooming-in, unless there is a medical reason for infant-mother separation.

If someone wants to take you baby to the nursery, you have every right to decline. If there's *ever* anything in the hospital being done that you do not want to be done, just state, "no thank you. I will kindly sign the refusal papers for [intervention] if you need me to for legal purposes."

Even if it is the hospital's protocol, you are under no obligation to follow ANY protocol and you have every right to refuse or decline any intervention.

With that being said, hospital protocols are there for a reason and (hopefully) they are using updated evidence-based research. Just ask for reasons, alternatives, risks, and benefits to make an informed decision for yourself and for your baby. Remember to use the BRAIN acronym for informed decision making – Benefits, Risks, Alternatives, Intuition, and Now or Never?

NEWBORN TESTING

NEWBORN SCREENING TEST: At 24 hours of age, your baby will undergo a state-mandated newborn screening test, AKA the "PKU test" which tests for 80 rare metabolic diseases. The goal of the program is to identify babies with these genetic metabolic disorders early, so treatment can be started right away. This test is a send-out test, meaning you will get the results back in a few weeks and the results will be sent to your pediatrician. This is why it's important to choose a follow-up pediatrician before you have your baby, because they will be the one to follow-up with you if this testing is abnormal.

During the test, 6 circles on a piece of paper are filled with drops of your baby's blood. The nurse will prick your baby's heel with a lancet and collect the drips by squeezing your baby's foot. Usually, if baby is swaddled tightly and given a pacifier with sweet-ease (sugar water used during painful procedures), they don't show any signs of pain and don't even cry. Alternatively, you can hold your baby skin-to-skin or breastfeed your baby while this screen is being done and that can have the same (if not better) comforting effects. You can decline this test for religious regions, but pros generally outweigh cons. Scan for more information about the test in California.

Information may differ depending on the state you are in.

CCHD TEST: In addition, your baby will undergo a CCHD Screen (Critical Congenital Heart Defect Screen) after 24 hours of age. During this test, a small oxygen-monitoring probe (like the one we put on your finger when we take your vital signs) is placed on their right hand/wrist and right foot and their oxygen saturation is monitored for 5 minutes. We watch to make sure the pre-ductal oxygenation (right hand) is within 3 percentage points of the post-ductal oxygenation (right foot) and is >95%. Babies with low oxygenation are at a higher risk for CHD's and would normally have an echocardiogram (ultrasound picture of the heart & non-invasive) to take a closer look at the heart structures.

JAUNDICE TEST: Generally, your baby's jaundice level will usually be checked at 24 hours of age. This is normally assessed with a transcutaneous bilirubin meter (TcB) or a blood draw. The TcB is noninvasive and is basically a small handheld machine which flashes light at your baby's chest and tells us how much bilirubin is built up in your baby's body AKA level of jaundice AKA yellowing of the skin – refer to the chapter on Jaundice for more information.)

WEIGHT: Most hospitals will weigh your baby at 24 hours of age, or before discharge from the hospital. Remember, it is normal for your baby to lose weight at this time. If you received excessive IV fluids through labor, this could be a major contributing factor to your baby's weight loss. For healthy, term newborns it can be completely normal to lose 7-10% of birth weight in those first few days, but baby should be back to birth weight by 2 weeks old.

SAFE SLEEP

It's important to know safe sleep guidelines for your newborn. In the US, approximately 3500 infants die each year from sleep-related deaths. The American Association of Pediatrics (AAP) sets guidelines for safe sleep based on current research, to reduce the chance of SIDS (Sudden Infant Death Syndrome) or suffocation. These guidelines follow the A B C's – ALONE, BACK, CRIB. To read the full AAP 2022 guidelines, visit the link.

But did you know 60-75% of breastfeeding mommas end up co-sleeping, whether on purpose or accidentally? The La Leche League states if you are: A nonsmoker, sober and unimpaired, a breastfeeding mother AND your baby is: healthy and full-term, on his back, lightly dressed AND you both are: on a safe surface, THEN your baby in bed with you is at no greater risk for SIDS than if he's nearby in a crib. These safe sleep guidelines are known as "The Safe Sleep Seven" and can be viewed at the link to the right.

One of the big reasons bedsharing is safer when you're breastfeeding is the way you position your body next to your baby. During sleep, you'll automatically go into the same position as breastfeeding mothers all over the world and throughout time. It's called a "cuddle curl," and its nature's way of protecting a baby during sleep. With you curled on your side in the fetal position around your baby, your knees come up and your arm tucks under your head or pillow, or curls around your baby, creating a protected space. There's no way for you to roll toward your baby because your bent legs won't let you. And no one else can roll into the space because your knees and elbows are in the way.

A bedside sleeper is a great alternative that allows for both easy access to the breast AND limiting co-sleeping. Bedside sleepers are bassinettes with three sides and **open** on the side next to your bed, so baby is separate from you, yet in proximity for breastfeeding. Imagine you have to grab your crying baby from their crib in the middle of the night to feed them. Do you really want to wake up, get out of bed, grab the baby, get back into bed, breastfeed them, get back up, put them back into their crib without waking them, then walk back to your own bed to go back to sleep? No, believe me, you won't. If you have a cesarean section, this will be virtually impossible to do immediately after delivery due to the incision. Bedside sleepers at the same level as your mattress are lifesavers because you can easily reach over to grab your baby, rather than getting up or having to reach into a walled-off bassinet. The best bedside sleepers only have 3 sides, a short lip on the fourth side, or have a zipper that can be unzipped to access your baby.

Whichever sleeping arrangement you choose, it is recommended to keep baby in your room, but not in your bed for at least the first 6 months of life.

Many mothers still choose to co-sleep for the first few months after delivery, just make an informed and safe decision that is right for your family and do your research ahead of time. The key points for safe sleep for all babies: Stay smoke-free. Stay sober. Stay off sofas, upholstered chairs, and recliners for sleep. Keep your healthy baby lightly dressed, on his back, and near you for sleep. And, of course, keep breastfeeding.

SIDS

Sudden Infant Death Syndrome (SIDS) is a term used to describe the sudden death of an infant less than 1 year old without a known cause, even after investigation. While the cause is unknown, SIDS is associated with the inability of a baby to arouse from sleep and is highest risk for babies 2-6 months of age.

Here are some general things to do to reduce the chance of SIDS.

- Always place your baby on their back to sleep.
- Use a *firm* mattress in a safety-approved crib.
- Have a fan running in your baby's room.
- No soft, fluffy bedding, toys, or pillows in the baby's sleep area.
- Breastfeeding is recommended - unless medically contraindicated, mothers should breastfeed exclusively (or feed with expressed milk) for at least six months.
- Room-in with your infant at home: in the parents' room, but in his/her own crib or basinet, ideally for the first year of life, but at least for the first six months. Evidence exists that infants who sleep in their parents' room, in their own cribs, have a decreased risk of SIDS of as much as 50%.
- Pacifier at nap time and bedtime once breastfeeding has been established (4-6

weeks old). It does not need to be reinserted once the infant falls asleep/falls out
- Do *not* allow any smoking near or around your baby.
- Avoid alcohol and illicit drug use during pregnancy and after birth.
- Dress your baby in what you are wearing. Do not over bundle or cover the face or head (avoid hats).
- Avoid the use of commercial devices that are inconsistent with safe sleep recommendations, especially devices that claim to reduce the risk of SIDS. Examples include but are not limited to monitoring socks, wedges and positioners or other devices placed in the adult bed for to separate the infant from others in the bed.
- Do not use home cardiorespiratory monitors as a strategy to reduce the risk of SIDS.
- Supervised, awake tummy time.
- Swaddling is not recommended as a strategy to reduce SIDS risk. If infants are swaddled, they should always be placed on their back. Swaddling should be snug around the chest but allow for room at the hips and knees. When an infant shows signs of attempting to roll, swaddling should no longer be used.

BENEFITS OF BREASTFEEDING

Firstly, the previous chapter on SIDS may have been scary to read. But it may comfort you to know, babies who are breastfed have a lower risk for SIDS compared to babies who were never fed breastmilk.

Chances are, if you are reading this book, you are already planning and wanting to breastfeed. Maybe you are a first-time mom or maybe you have done this before. Either way, I am here for you on your journey, wherever it may find you.

So, what is the benefit of breastfeeding? To summarize: **Breastmilk is the best thing for your baby's health and development.** Breastmilk is much more than just nutrition and food; it is a biologically active substance that aids in optimal growth and development of organs, gut, immunity, and overall health for the rest of your child's life. It aids in growth and development and decreases the risk of disease.

Breastfeeding is the communication between a mother's immune system and her baby. Breastmilk is made by your body specifically *for your baby* and adapts to what your baby needs on a minute-to-minute basis. When you kiss or feed your baby, there is feedback of information that changes the composition of your breast milk in response to the environment and your baby's needs. For example, if your baby is sick, your baby's saliva backflows through the nipple and into the breasts in retrograde milk flow and the milk will respond to the baby's saliva. There is even a specific feedback loop called the Enteromammary pathway where specific antigen protection has been discovered in response to a baby's environment. For example, if a mother detects a virus in the baby's environment, a signal is sent to Peyer's patches in mom's gut which then sends antibodies through the lymphatic system to the breastmilk to protect the baby. WOW!

Breastmilk acts as your baby's immune system before their immune system is fully mature. Your breastmilk provides components such as immunoglobulins, lactoferrin, and oligosaccharides for immune support and maturation. These and other proteins found in breastmilk not only protect against infection and inflammation, but they also aid in organ development and a healthy microbiome. Babies who are breastfed have a lower risk of asthma, obesity, type 1 diabetes, ear infections, and SIDS.

Without making this a textbook and getting too scientific on you, here are some other examples of how your milk changes and supports your baby.

- Preterm milk has more fats = brain food
- Foremilk (at the start of a feeding) has more lactose = brain growth
- Hindmilk (at the end of a feeding) has more fat = weight gain
- Macronutrients give your baby calories to survive.

- Micronutrients such as vitamins, minerals, nucleotides, probiotics, and prebiotics are present for your baby to thrive.
- Stem cells are present and become other types of cells.
- Bifidus factors aid in the growth of healthy gut flora (good bacteria like Lactobacillus)
- Oligosaccharides act as decoys for bad bacteria and flood the GI tract of your baby.
- Lysozyme damages bacterial cell walls and is anti-inflammatory (3x more prominent in human milk than cow milk).
- Erythropoietin is abundant in breastmilk and increases RBC's and aids in immunology.
- Leukocytes help your baby resist infection by phagocytosis (eating) pathogens.
- Host resistance factors such as gangliosides, interferon, B12 binding protein, prostaglandins, ribonuclease, etc. are also present for immune support.
- Epidermal growth factor (also found in amniotic fluid) heals and coats baby's GI tract and is highest in early milk and at the end of lactation.

Research about breastmilk is ongoing and we are constantly discovering more benefits. For example, one of the factors of breastmilk Human alpha lactalbumin may combine with oleic acid in your baby's stomach and intestines and creates HAMLET which is which is lethal to tumor cells!

The process of making milk begins in pregnancy; your body is biologically programmed to be able to provide for your baby as soon as they are born. This process is hormone driven as it is after the birth of your baby and delivery of the placenta.

For you, breastfeeding reduces the risk of breast cancer, ovarian cancer, type 2 diabetes, postpartum depression, and high blood pressure and the longer you breastfeed, the lower these risks get.

Also, your breasts are always with you, you don't have to cart around formula and bottles for your baby when you leave the house. Breastfeeding is much more convenient because you can feed anytime, anywhere as long as your baby is with you.

All in all, breastfeeding is a mutually beneficial relationship between baby and mom. It supports newborn secure attachment and fulfills your baby's needs to be held, cuddled, and nurtured. Breastmilk is the best source of nutrition for your baby and is designed for their growth and development.

COLOSTRUM

Around week 15-20 of pregnancy, your body begins the production of colostrum, so it is present before your baby is born. Colostrum is also known as "pre-milk" or "liquid gold," because it is a small volume, but highly concentrated (not a lot of water) and is only present for the first ~3 days after delivery before transitioning to more dilute mature milk. Colostrum is usually very thick consistency like honey and generally clear or yellow to orange in color.

Colostrum is present in small volumes because it coats and protects your baby's GI tract, and your baby's stomach is only about the size of a blueberry in the first few days of life! When you compare a few drips of colostrum to a blueberry, you only need a few drips to fill the whole volume of the blueberry.

Colostrum is all your baby needs in these first few days of life.

You have probably heard women say, "I'm waiting for my milk to come in" or "my milk isn't in yet." What they actually mean is they have not seen a large increase in milk volume yet (the mature milk) and they still have colostrum.

On day 3-5 (ish) after delivery, you will notice a large volume increase of your milk supply as your colostrum transitions into "mature milk." The mature milk is thinner in consistency and has more of a "milky" white appearance than colostrum.

HAND EXPRESSION

It is recommended to hand express a minimum of 5 times per day, for at least 5 minutes, for the first 5 days after delivery to increase milk supply (in addition to breastfeeding). To learn how to hand express, watch the video in the QR code shown to the right.

The basics of hand expression are to press back into the breast, compress your fingers together, and then relax your hand. To collect the colostrum, express onto a spoon and then feed that directly to your baby via spoon-feeding. Alternatively, you can pull the colostrum into a small syringe from the spoon and save it to syringe/finger feed it to your baby at the next feed.

Hand expression is a great skill to know and utilize throughout your breastfeeding journey. You will always have your hands with you, even if you don't have your baby or a pump!

You can also add hand expression to your breastfeeding or pumping sessions to increase "emptying" of your breasts. This is called "hands-on" breastfeeding and pumping. Remember, breasts are never fully "empty" because they are constantly refilling as they empty out, so hand expression while breastfeeding or pumping just increases supply because they increase output!

ANTENATAL COLOSTRUM HARVESTING

Hand expression can be used prior to delivery when you are full term (and your healthcare provider says it's safe) to collect colostrum and save it for after delivery – this is known as antenatal colostrum harvesting. If your OBGYN or healthcare provider is against antenatal colostrum harvesting, use the BRAIN acronym to make an informed decision.

The usual arguments against hand expression in pregnancy is it could stimulate pre-term or early labor. However, the placenta is still secreting progesterone while you are pregnant, which inhibits oxytocin production, thus preventing pre-term birth. Also, nipple stimulation such as with breastfeeding older children while pregnant is NOT restricted, how is that any different from 5 minutes of hand expression?

You can buy syringes to save the colostrum from online sites such as Amazon. Just make sure you label them with the date and time they were expressed and freeze them. You can layer/collect colostrum for 4 days in the fridge, but store in the freezer after 4 days. Bring these syringes with you to the hospital (on ice) and give them to the L&D nurses to put into the refrigerator when you arrive. Once the colostrum thaws out from being frozen, it is only good in the refrigerator for 24 hours, be mindful of this because you do not want to waste it. You can keep them frozen in a cooler on ice, or only bring a few syringes at a time to the hospital. You can feed these syringes of colostrum to your baby after delivery to increase the volume they are getting. This is especially beneficial if your baby goes to the NICU, is small for gestational age, has jaundice, has low blood sugars, or is separated from you for any reason.

BREASTMILK STORAGE

The Human Milk Banking Association of North America (HMBANA) is the gold standard for breast milk storage. Their guidelines differ slightly from the CDC and Academy of Breastfeeding Medicine Protocol #8.

To make storage guidelines easy to remember, I have simplified it into an easy rule – "the rule of FOURS."

THE RULE OF FOURS: Breast milk is stable *four*...

4 hours at room temp

4 days in the refrigerator

4 months in the freezer (but up to 1 year+ in a deep freezer)

CDC Guidelines article

ABM Protocol #8 article:

Here is my simplified video explaining these breast milk storage guidelines, so they are easier to remember:

BREASTMILK COMPOSITION

In the animal kingdom, breastmilk composition varies between species based on how often they need to feed their babies – how often they visit the nest for some and how far they walk for others.

Carry mammals (apes, marsupials) are mammals that carry their young. They feed approximately every 30 minutes, and they have the lowest composition of fat and highest composition of carbs found in their milk. If you think about carbs as being quick energy and fat as long-term energy, you can see how often each of these mammal mothering styles differ based on their milk composition.

In contrast to carry animals, cache animals have the most fat found in their milk and the least amount of carbs. This tells us their babies can go long periods of time between feeds. These cache animals such as deer and rabbits often leave their young in a safe place for 12 hours at a time.

Now, look at the composition of human milk in comparison to the other types of mammals in the table on the next page.

How often do you think humans need to feed their babies based on the composition of human breastmilk? What type of mammal mothering style do humans have? What does this mean for how often you need to feed your baby?

Type of mammal mothering style	Examples of mammals	How often they feed their babies	Milk composition by volume
Carry	Apes, marsupials	~ Every 30 minutes	4% fat 2.1% protein 6% carbs
Follow	Goats, giraffes	~ Every 2 hours	Varied fat 5% protein 5% carbs
Nesting	Dogs, pigs, cats	~ Every 4 hours	8-9% fat 5-10% protein 3-4% carbs
Cache	Deer, rabbits	~ Every 12 hours	12-31% fat 10% protein 0.5-1% carbs
Humans	YOU	?	3.5-4% fat 0.9-1% protein 7% carbs

If you said humans are carry animals, you are correct. Human babies need to be carried and near their mothers. They are meant to be fed at least every 2-3 hours and on demand. Human milk is highest in lactose (carbs) and lowest in protein. Human milk is quick to digest, which is why human babies must be fed often. We are meant to feed our babies 8-12 times per day and on demand with hunger cues. We are meant to nurse around the clock.

About 40% of the calories in your breastmilk are carbohydrates in the form of lactose. When people learn there is lactose in their milk, they immediately fear a "lactose intolerance." But **your baby cannot be allergic to your milk.** When you hear the phrase lactose intolerance it is not actually lactose that babies have an allergy to, **it is a cow milk protein allergy.** Your baby *can* be allergic to cow milk protein called beta lactoglobulin which is not naturally found in human milk *unless* mom consumes cow's milk. When mom consumes cow's milk, this protein is absorbed and leaked into her breastmilk. When present in breastmilk, this cow milk protein *can* cause allergies and sensitivities in babies.

Fat makes up about 4% of your breastmilk but is about 50% of the calories. The types of fat in breastmilk, but not the amounts, vary based on your diet. For example, eating more fat in your diet does not cause an increase *amount* of fat in your breastmilk. However, eating healthy fats (such as omega 3 and 6) does change the *type* of fats found in your breastmilk and is beneficial for your baby's brain development.

Fat content of breastmilk is more dependent on the emptiness of the breasts and mechanical compression rather than your diet; the degree of emptiness of the breasts is what drives the fat. Think of your breasts as making fatty milk when they are empty and less fat when they are full (more dilute). If you've heard someone say, "I make fatty milk" or, "my breastmilk is skim-milk," these comments are not valid because the fat composition in breastmilk is dynamic based on what the baby needs and changes throughout the feeding.

As the breasts empty during a feed, the fat content of the milk steadily increases. At the end of a feeding, the breastmilk is called the hindmilk, which is highest in fat content. This hindmilk can be thought of as "dessert" that keeps your baby fuller, longer.

For more information on breastmilk composition, macronutrients in breastmilk, and milk composition between species of animals, visit the QR codes below.

CASE STUDY: An exclusively breastfeeding mother was concerned she "might not be giving her baby what he needs" because her baby had fallen off his growth curve (he was a negative percentile on the WHO Growth Charts that we use as a standard to measure optimal weight gain). The baby was no longer gaining weight according to his "percentile." Her pediatrician told her to begin supplementing with formula 2-3 times per day because her breastmilk was not "fatty enough" for her baby and not giving "the density" her baby needed to gain weight.

She was exclusively breastfeeding up until that point but doubted her body's ability to provide for her baby after the comment from the pediatrician. Is it her milk composition limiting her baby's weight gain? Would formula be medically necessary at this point?

After investigating her breastfeeding patterns, it turned out she was feeding on both breasts during a feeding for about 10 minutes each, rather finishing the first breast first. Remember, fuller breasts (think more dilute) have less fat content than empty breasts (at the end of a feeding). She also was going 6-8 hours between feedings at night because her baby was sleeping, and she was not waking him to feed. During the day, she only fed about every 3 hours if her baby was crying rather than feeding with early hunger cues. All these things can contribute to slow weight gain and should be thoroughly assessed before advising a new mom to start formula. She did not want to supplement with formula, but the pediatrician told her she needs to for her baby to gain weight.

What would you do in this scenario? What should the pediatrician have done differently? What is best for the baby? Scenarios like these are not uncommon.

In other aspects of life, when we have a problem that requires a specialist, we go to see a specialist. If we have a heart problem, we go to see a cardiologist rather than your PCP. If we have a problem with the electrical on our house, we use an electrician rather than a general contractor. The same goes for breastfeeding. If we have a problem with breastfeeding, why don't we go to see the specialist who specializes in breastfeeding?

BREASTFEEDING & LATCHING

When you are breastfeeding, the latch is everything. A latch is when your baby attaches their mouth around your nipple and areola during a feeding session. If the baby's mouth is not wide enough or the nipple is not far enough into your baby's mouth, we call that a shallow latch. In order to properly empty the breast, your baby needs to have a deep latch with as much of the nipple and areola into their mouth as possible.

Babies use their mouth to both compress and suction the breast, which is why we need both the nipple and areola in their mouth. While properly latched, the baby's tongue uses a wave-like motion to massage the areola while negative pressure from suction pulls the milk through the ducts in the nipple. Nipples are not straws and do not function as such which is why babies cannot empty the breast if they are only latched to the tip of the nipple.

There are many breastfeeding positions to latch your baby in, but the most common are cradle, cross-cradle, football, side-lying, laid-back, and Australian holds. Some moms prefer to only feed in one or two of these positions, whereas others are comfortable feeding in any and all positions. The most important aspect of any breastfeeding hold is that milk is being emptied from the breast and into baby. This transfer of milk from mom to baby is called milk exchange. When your baby is latched properly in a deep latch, their lips will be flanged out like ducky lips and their latch will be asymmetrical with more of their mouth covering the bottom half of the areola below the nipple. This asymmetrical latch is very important because if the baby is latched with the nipple straight into their mouth, the tongue will massage the nipple in the wave-like motion rather than the areola. If this happens, the nipple will be compressed by the tongue onto the roof of the baby's mouth and will cause nipple damage and decreased milk exchange.

Imagine the breast as a tree and the nipple as the tree trunk. The milk producing sacs in the breast are the leaves while the branches of the tree are all the ducts within the breast. All of the branches of the tree (the ducts) combine into the main trunk (the nipple) to empty the milk from the breast. If the nipple is compressed or pinched from a shallow latch like a pinched hose, then the milk from the breast cannot be emptied. If the breast is left full for a prolonged amount of time, signals are sent to the milk producing sacs (the leaves) to reduce the production of milk and your supply decreases. If this shallow latch happens repetitively, milk supply will slowly decrease as the breasts are not effectively emptied.

THREE RULES FOR LATCHING:

In any breastfeeding position, there are only 3 main rules to obtaining a deep, asymmetrical latch. These three rules are:

1. **Tummy-to-tummy**
   - Have your baby's spine aligned so their tummy is facing you and so is their face/mouth. You do not want your baby's tummy facing to the ceiling and head turned towards you, which is hard to swallow.
2. **Nose-to-nipple**
   - By aiming your baby's nose at your nipple, the lower lip should be placed on the BOTTOM of the areola, creating an asymmetrical latch. Think about how you take a bit of a hamburger or a big bite of sandwich – the lower lip hits first and then the mouth comes over the bite like an arch.
3. **Baby-to-breast**
   - Support your baby behind the shoulder blades with your thumb and fingers just below their ears.
   - Always bring your baby towards you, rather than chasing your baby with your breast. The chin should touch the breast first when latching, with the bottom lip touching near/on the bottom rim of your areola. Then, the mouth scoops and latches over the nipple.
   - Your baby should be brought to the natural position your breast sits, even if they are low.

If you use these three rules, you will *almost always* obtain a deep, asymmetrical latch, which is necessary for milk removal from the breast. If the latch is shallow or symmetrical and pinching, the milk will not be emptied effectively from the breast.

There are so many other things to say about breastfeeding (this is why I offer consultations and prenatal education) but I have created a list below of the basics to a successful breastfeeding experience.

Refer back to these breastfeeding basics frequently and as needed throughout your breastfeeding journey.

BREASTFEEDING BASICS:

- Feed at least every 2-3 hours (maximum amount of time between feeds, from the start of the first to the start of the next) during the day.
- A general rule of thumb is to feed **at least** 8-12 times in 24 hours **and on demand** with signs of hunger (ends up being at least every 2 hours during the day and every 4 hours at night). You will probably be feeding much more frequent than this if you are really feeding on demand. That is NORMAL.
- Feed your baby with early signs of hunger: rooting, licking, searching for the nipple, more alert, etc.
- If you feed you baby before they are HANGRY, it will be easier to latch.

- Try not to go longer than 3-4 hours without milk removal because overly full breasts cause slower milk production/milk stasis/clogged ducts/mastitis (do not go more than 5 hours at night).
- Write down the number of times you feed for the first few weeks, use an app if it's easier to keep track. This will ensure you are feeding the minimum number of times per day.
- Drain each breast thoroughly <u>at least</u> once per day.
- **Offer both breasts for each feeding, burping between breasts. In the first few days, if the second breast is not emptied because baby is too tired, hand express on that side and supplement the expressed breast milk to your baby via spoon or syringe.**
- Feed the first breast as the full "dinner" and try to empty the breast. Then, offer the second as a "dessert." It's ok if they don't want to feed on the second breast, just offer this second breast first for the next feed. By doing this, your supply will stay stable or slightly decrease on this second side based on this decrease in demand. To increase supply, use your Haakaa (or hand express/pump) on the second breast to increase demand. Either way, offer this breast *first* for the next feeding and alternate.
- The hind milk (milk at the end of a feed) has the most fat.

- High-volume mature milk generally "comes in" day 3-5 but may be later.
- Make sure your latch is not pinching or painful.
- If you have a painful latch, break the latch by putting your finger into the side of your baby's mouth to break the suction, pull baby away, then try again.
- Build a pillow nest around you (before latching) to support your arms and baby while feeding or use a nursing support pillow like the Boppy or My Brest Friend. This can help if you're struggling with supporting your baby's weight in your hand.
- Your baby's chin should touch the breast first and the baby's chest should be pulled close to your body when latched.
- Hold your breast in a C or U shape depending on the breastfeeding position. You want to compress or "sandwich" the breast small enough to fit BOTH nipple and areola into your baby's mouth (like we squish down a hamburger/sandwich to take a big bite)

See video here on how to compress the breast for an asymmetrical, deep latch.

HOW TO LATCH:

- Utilize the three rules for latching: nose-to-nipple, tummy-to-tummy, baby-to-breast.

- Position baby's nose aimed at your nipple and tummy aimed at your tummy facing the breast.
- Baby's hands should be surrounding the breast like they are hugging the breast, not tucked between their body and your chest.
- Support your baby's neck and shoulder blades when trying to latch, holding right below the ears rather than on the back of the head.
- Gently rub/swipe/tickle your nipple down baby's mouth (from nose to chin) to have them open wide.
- Gently guide your baby onto your breast when they have a wide-open mouth (>140 degrees) 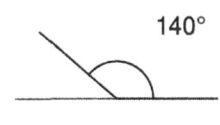
- Bring your baby to the breast gently, pulling them toward you, not the breast to baby.
- Use the **asymmetrical latching technique** shown below to prevent sore nipples. Do not latch symmetrically onto the nipple. More of your areola should be showing on the top of your latch by the baby's nose. Little to no areola should be visible below your baby's bottom lip. The bottom lip should be touching on or near the rim of your areola (depending on how large your areolas are).

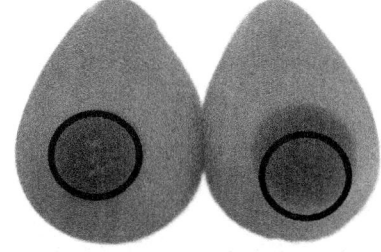

- A deep latch should feel like a tugging sensation, not like a pinch.
- If you have sore or damaged nipples, you may feel pain when baby first latches on, but this SHOULD go away in the first few seconds of the feed, if it doesn't, break the latch and try again.
- If a latch was painful or feels "pinchy," look at your nipple after you break the latch. The nipple should still look round. If it doesn't look round, see the table below.
- For latching difficulties, see the table below in "LATCHNG PROBLEMS" and please make an appointment to see a Lactation Consultant.

Video showing a "good" latch:

SIGNS OF A GOOD FEEDING

- Consistent suck, brief pauses to swallow or breathe.
- Hearing swallowing (once mature milk is in)
- Wide open mouth, most of nipple and areola in the mouth
- Deep, strong pulling or tugging, no sharp pain
- Vigorous sucking
- Lips flanged out.
- Breasts are soft after feeding.
- Seeing milk in/on baby's mouth
- Feeling a "let-down" reflex or change in baby's feeding rhythm.
- Adequate number of wet and poopy diapers
- Minimal weight loss
- Baby regains birth weight by 2 weeks old and ¾ to 1 oz per day after

SIGNS OF A POOR FEEDING

- Feeling pain during feeding
- Inconsistent or weak suck (fluttering)
- Shallow or narrow mouth, baby kissing nipple
- Difficulty latching and staying latched (popping off)
- Clicking or popping sounds
- Lips tucked under

- Prolonged nursing (>25 minutes on each side)
- Infrequent nursing, baby does not wake to feed every 2-3 hours.
- Baby is not satisfied at the end of feeding from both breasts.
- Engorgement
- Inadequate number of wet and poopy diapers
- Rapid or excessive weight loss (>7-10%) during the first few days
- Has not regained birth weight by 2 weeks.
- Slow weight gain (< ½ – ¾ oz per day)

BREASTFEEDING POSITIONS

The strategies for latching shown above are based on mother-led feeding positions. Mother-led means you are actively assisting your baby in obtaining a latch. In doing so, you should **not** be using a "ready, aim, RAM" technique to latching or forcefully pushing baby's head *into* your breast. Instead, think of the latch as gentle guidance *onto* the breast. These mother-led breastfeeding include but are not limited to the football hold, cradle, cross-cradle, koala, dangle, and side-lying.

There are also techniques for latching based on baby-led breastfeeding positions. This means, baby is taking the lead and you allow baby to self-latch to the breast. This can be done in many positions where baby is not fighting gravity to latch. Positions include but are not limited to the reclined or laid-back hold, koala (AKA Australian), and side-lying.

There are many positions to breastfeed in, but these are the basics to get you started. There are *no* incorrect positions to breastfeed in if you have a deep, successful latch.

Cradle hold: Mother supports the baby's head on her *forearm*

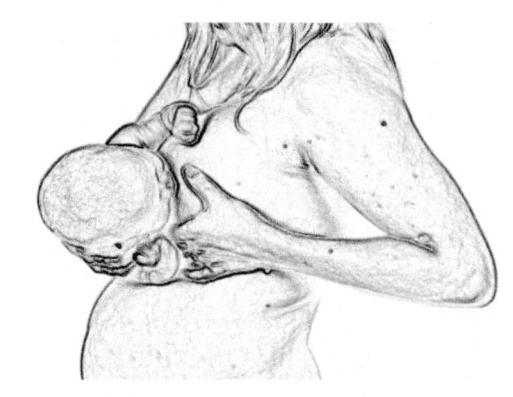

Cross-cradle hold

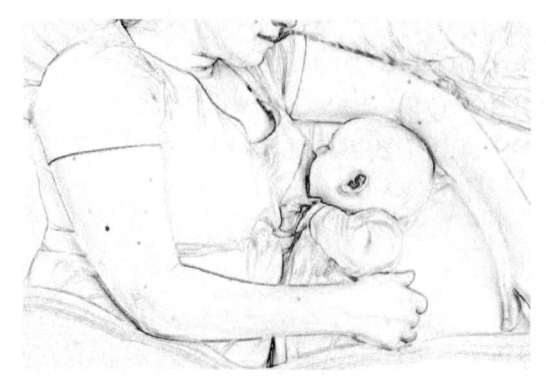

Side-lying breastfeeding hold shown in bed. Also demonstrating the "cuddle curl."

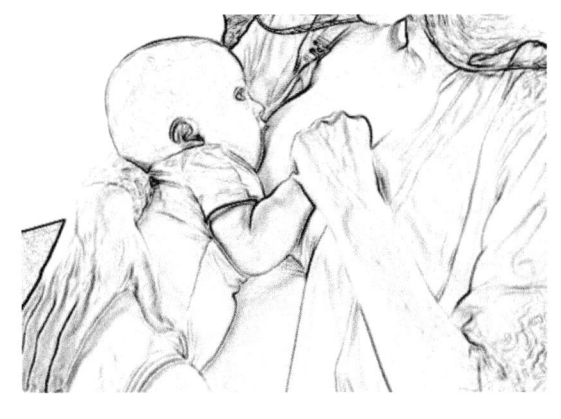

Laid-back AKA reclined breastfeeding hold. If baby is straddling mom's leg, this could be called the koala hold.

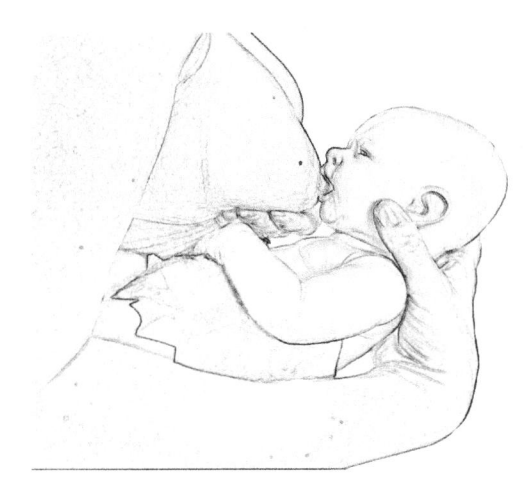

Football hold, AKA Rugby-ball hold.

Scan the QR code to see more breastfeeding positions.

FEEDING ON DEMAND

Yes, babies feed "every 2 to 3 hours," but this is the **maximum** time between feeds (from the start of one feed to the start of the next). Also, one feeding session could last up to an hour, but usually averages 10-20 minutes or so. What does that mean for you? You'll be feeding a LOT in the beginning following your baby's cues, but this will establish a supply based on your baby's needs.

It is important to feed you baby on demand by watching your baby rather than watching the clock.

Feed your baby with early sings of hunger when they are not hangry. If they get too hungry (HANGRY) they will be difficult to latch and maintain a latch. Remember, crying is a *late* sign of hunger.

EARLY SIGNS OF HUNGER INCLUDE:

- rooting (opening mouth and searching for the breast with mouth open)
- actively awake and alert, looking around
- smacking lips/tongue
- increased alertness
- sucking on hands
- head turning to find the breast
- opening and closing mouth

If your baby is showing early hunger cues, disregard WHEN they last ate and instead just get them back onto the breast. For example, you just finished feeding your baby 30 minutes ago, but they're awake now and looking around. Get them back onto the breast.

Watch your baby, not the clock.

If you are feeding on demand, you may be feeding as often as every half hour at first. The time between feeds will gradually increase as your baby's stomach size grows and your milk volume increases. This means your baby can eat more volume at each feeding session less frequently rather than less volume more frequently.

MILK SUPPLY

Milk supply is based on supply and demand; the more *frequently* and *effectively* the breasts are emptied, the *more* milk you will produce. If your breasts are not emptied enough or often enough, your milk supply will decrease. Your milk volume and composition are dynamic, meaning they are constantly changing based on your baby's needs and how much the breasts are *emptied*.

Stimulating "empty" breasts is what tells your body to make more milk.

Think of your breasts as an ice machine. As ice is emptied and used from the ice machine, more ice is made to fill the ice machine back up. Breast milk is the same way; the more the breasts are emptied, the more milk is made to keep up with the demand.

Always follow your baby's early hunger cues by feeding as often as they cue (may be 8-16+ times per day), but always wake your baby to eat **at least** 8-12 times in 24 hours. This is called feeding "on-demand."

TIPS FOR MAINTAINING SUPPLY:

- Keep your baby close to you and "wear your baby" as much as possible to feed on-demand anytime your infant shows signs of hunger AKA early hunger cues.

- Deep, asymmetrical latch that is not painful or pinchy.
- Wake your baby to eat **at least** 8-12 times in 24 hours.
- Empty each breast thoroughly at least once per day and offer both breasts at each feeding.
- Try not to go longer than 3-4 hours without milk removal because over-full breasts cause slower milk production (max 5 hours at night).
- Delay the use of a pacifier until breastfeeding is well established (4-6 weeks).
- Avoid things that are known to reduce milk supply: Smoking, Birth control pills and injections, Decongestants, antihistamines (such as Benadryl), Severe weight loss diets, Excessive amounts of mints, parsley, or sage.

TIPS TO INCREASE SUPPLY:

Triple feeding is a technique where you breastfeed first to allow baby to empty your breasts, then pump to empty them completely, then supplement with this expressed breast milk at the next feeding. This can be a LOT of work, but it does work. You can also increase the frequency of pumping/breastfeeding to increase your supply.

Use a Haakaa on the opposite breast while your baby is latched and actively feeding. By using the

Haakaa at the same time you are breastfeeding, your body releases increased levels of Oxytocin and Prolactin hormones which increase milk supply and output. This technique "tricks" your body into thinking you are feeding two babies at the same time (this is the same reason why you always want to pump on both breasts at the same time when pumping.) While your Haakaa is in place, hand express and massage the breast with the Haakaa. Then, when your baby finishes on one side of your breasts, switch sides of both your baby and the Haakaa. You can start by doing this just once per day or do it with each feeding.

Hand expression in the first few days after delivery has been shown to increase supply. The current recommendation is to hand express 5 minutes/5 times per day for the first 5 days postpartum (in addition to breastfeeding) to increase milk supply. It is generally recommended to wait to start pumping until your milk supply and breastfeeding is well established (around 4-6 weeks). That way, your supply is based on what your baby needs.

Adjust your latch to be sure it is a deep, asymmetrical latch. See a lactation consultant to get minor adjustments that could make all the difference.

Power Pumping is a technique to simulate cluster feeding. You would pump for 20 minutes, then pause 10 min, then pump 10, then pause 10, etc. for an hour. Do this once per day for 2-3 days.

Try to get in "one more feeding" before you go to sleep, even if you must wake the baby.

Empty your breasts well by massaging while the baby is feeding or while you are pumping. This is called hands-on feeding or hands-on pumping.

PERCEIVED LOW SUPPLY

There is something to be said about your *perception* of your milk supply. It is very important to know what a low supply looks like and that it is surprisingly **rare to have a low supply** if you are feeding on demand. Most of the time, it's a PERCIEVED low supply, meaning mom thinks she has a low supply when in reality the supply is exactly what baby needs.

Often, moms think they have a low supply when they do not feel their breasts are engorged or hard especially between feeds.

Stimulating "empty" breasts is what tells your body to make more milk. Read that again. It's all supply and demand.

It is important to trust your body when you are breastfeeding, especially exclusively breastfeeding without pumping. Since you cannot see the milk coming out of the breast and into baby, it is easy to doubt yourself and think "baby is not getting enough." Remember, if your baby is having adequate poops and pees (output) per day and gaining weight (after the NORMAL initial weight loss) based on their growth curve, then your baby is getting enough. If you are properly feeding on demand, you are watching your baby's hunger cues rather than watching the clock and your milk supply will be based on your baby's needs.

Read more about the growth curve in the chapter on Newborn Weight Gain

CLUSTER FEEDING

Babies often feed frequently, in bunches during growth spurts, evenings, and in the first few days of life. This frequent pattern of breastfeeding is called cluster feeding and it's your baby's natural way to gain weight and increase your milk supply.

In the first few days of life, cluster feeding is your baby's way of telling your body to make milk. People will often mistake this cluster feeding pattern for a low milk supply, but that is not the case. Your baby is not feeding frequently because they are starving, it is quite the contrary. Your baby's frequent feeding pattern is what will determine your milk supply. Be wary of people who tell you your baby is "starving" when frequently feeding and fussy at the breast; in these first days of life, this is generally normal newborn behavior as your supply steadily increases to meet the demand.

Additionally, cluster feeding is common during growth spurts and when babies are learning new skills. These growth spurts are very common in the first year of life, typically around 3 weeks, 6 weeks, 3 months, and 6 months old, but can happen at anytime (every baby is different). These growth spurts usually last a few days and often cause your baby to breastfeed longer and more often to increase your milk supply. The more your baby breastfeeds, the more milk your body makes to keep up with their growing needs.

Also, during evenings, babies will often seem fussy and want to breastfeed more often than during the day. **Evening cluster feeding is normal newborn behavior and <u>does not</u> mean your baby isn't getting enough milk.** This is your baby's way of filling up their stomach before long stretches of sleep. Some babies will even do this every day, it can be totally normal.

Sometimes, stretches of cluster feeding mean feeding your baby every 15-30 minutes and that can be exhausting, **especially because they tend to also be fussy.** Your baby is not starving, this is normal newborn behavior. Remember, this is just temporary and it's your baby's way of increasing your milk supply and their intake.

The frequent feedings may cause you to question yourself – am I doing something wrong? Am I making enough milk? No, you aren't doing anything wrong, this is *normal* newborn behavior. And yes, you are making enough milk as long as your baby is gaining weight according to their growth curve. Continue to follow your baby's hunger cues, feed on demand, and monitor their weight trend. As you feed your baby more frequently, your body will adjust to make the right amount of milk. Trust your baby and your body.

AVERAGE MILK VOLUME

In the first day of life, your baby's stomach is estimated to be about the size of a blueberry. By day three, the stomach size grows to about the size of a cherry. Then, by day five, the baby's stomach is golf ball sized. At a month old, the infant's stomach is about the size of a large egg.

The funny thing about nature is that nothing is accidental.

Your milk supply in these first few days and weeks of your baby's life is based on their needs and correlates with the baby's stomach size, The following volumes are overly simplified estimates so you know what to expect, but milk volumes can vary greatly between people.

- On day one postpartum, you will generally see just *drops* of colostrum. This is NORMAL!
- Day 2 ~ 1tsp
- Day 3 ~ 1TBSP
- Day 4 ~ 1oz
- Day 5 ~ 1oz+
- By two weeks, you generally will be producing about 24oz in 24 hours (an approximate 1oz per hour throughout the day)

Again, these are just averages most people see in the first few weeks postpartum. I wanted to provide these, so you know what to expect, but it is very important to not dwell on these volumes, especially if you are exclusively breastfeeding on demand.

In the first few weeks of life, rather than concentrating on how much you can *see* coming out of the breast, monitor your baby's output (poops and pees) instead. After the first two weeks, try to regularly monitor weight gain according to their growth curve. On average, babies should gain approximately 1oz per day, once they reach 2 weeks old. Read more about weight gain in the Newborn Weight Gain chapter.

POOPS/PEES (OUTPUT)

In the first one to two weeks of life, monitoring output is the best way to track your baby's intake. If you are exclusively breastfeeding at the breast, you will not be able to visualize the volumes your baby is receiving from your breast which can be concerning for some moms because they worry "is my baby getting enough?" Alternatively, if you are pumping and monitoring volumes, this can be even more concerning to new moms because it is VERY small volumes at first, which is completely normal. This is why **monitoring output is a better indicator your baby is "getting enough" when compared to measuring milk volumes.**

Generally, the minimum number of poops and pees your baby should have each day correlates with days old. For example, on day 1 (first 24 hours of life), you baby should have a minimum of 1 poop and 1 pee for that day. Many babies have much more than that, but this is just the minimum. For day 2, baby should have 2 poops and 2 pees (minimum). On day 3, baby should have 3 poops and 3 pees (minimum). On day 4, baby should have 4 poops and 4 pees (minimum). Up until day 5, where baby should have a minimum of 5 poops and 5 pees per day and this will continue until about 8 weeks of life. After 8 weeks, it can vary greatly from baby to baby, so talk to your pediatrician about what they recommend.

It is important to keep track of your baby's output because it tells us your baby is eating enough. What goes *in* must come *out*! If your baby is meeting these minimums and gaining weight, **they <u>are</u> getting enough volume to eat**.

If you are exclusively breastfeeding, some babies CAN go a few days between poops, but this generally does not occur until after 8 weeks old. If your baby does not meet the minimum number of outputs per day, that is beyond the scope of "normal" for this book so please consult your pediatrician and an IBCLC (International Board-Certified Lactation Consultant) for any and all medical advice. This book is intended for educational purposes only and is not intended nor implied to be a substitute for medical advice.

Also, these minimums are just the general guidelines; your pediatrician may be following different guidelines. Always go with *your* pediatrician's recommendations (if you don't agree with them, maybe find a new Pediatrician).

Baby's poops should transition from the black, tarry meconium into a green, then yellow stool by day 5. If the stool is not yellow by day 5 of life, see a pediatrician immediately.

Here is a video explaining how many diapers your baby should have:

After the first one to two weeks of life, output is still important to monitor, but you do not need to write down every single poop, pee, and feed your baby has. Instead, monitoring weight gain is a much better indicator of your milk supply and your baby's feeding tendencies. Read more about this on the chapter "Newborn Weight Gain."

NEWBORN WEIGHT GAIN

Monitoring your baby's weight is one of the best indicators of a sufficient milk supply, once your mature milk volumes have been established around 7-14 days postpartum.

I **highly** recommend getting a baby scale changing pad to trend your baby's weight. They are about $100+ but are one of the only products for breastfeeding that will really benefit your experience, especially long term. Rather than tracking every feed, poop, and pee your baby has, you can instead weigh your baby once a day or every few days. This way of monitoring tracks your baby's growth over time, called a trend. We monitor trends because it shows your baby's specific growth on their "growth curve." This "growth curve" is basically a percentile of where your baby's weight is compared to other babies throughout the world using the World Health Organization (WHO) growth chart.

At each well-baby visit at the pediatrician's office, the doctor will review your baby's growth based on this WHO growth chart. These well-baby visits are usually every 2 months if everything is deemed "normal." However, if your infant is not gaining weight, this can be a long interval of time before a problem is identified. By using a scale at home, you can identify a problem and *intervene* before it becomes an issue.

In the first week of your baby's life, it is **normal** for them to lose up to 7-10% of their birth weight. This is because colostrum is a natural laxative and helps to eliminate the broken-down red blood cells and other waste from gestation. This elimination is important to reduce the risk of jaundice. Also, milk volumes are very low in the first few days to week of your baby's life as your volumes steadily increase based on your baby's stomach size and feeding frequency.

Once you see the large increase in milk volumes around day 3-5 postpartum as you transition to mature milk, your baby will start to gain weight. Your baby should be back to birth weight by two weeks of age. Then, after two weeks old, your baby should gain an average of 1oz per day. By six months old, your baby will normally double their birth wight. Then, by 1 year old, they should be approximately triple their birth weight.

In that first week of your baby's life, it can be concerning for a new mom to see their infant losing weight. This is why I do not generally recommend monitoring weight in this first week, before you have transitioned to mature milk volumes. Instead, remember to count the number of poops and pees your baby is having per day.

But what if your baby loses more than 7-10% of their birth weight? Sadly, that is out of the scope of this book, as every baby is different, and every mother is different. There are many contributing factors to why babies lose more than the recommended weight, which is why you should seek an IBCLC (International Board-Certified Lactation Consultant) assistance if this is the case. In this situation, a well-trained IBCLC will be able to explore the cause and find solutions to support your breastfeeding goals. Just remember to use your BRAIN acronym for making informed decisions, especially if formula supplementation is advised before trying other measures to supplement your baby with expressed breast milk.

NEWBORN SLEEP CYCLES

Eat, sleep, poop repeat, if that's all newborns do, then why is the newborn stage so hard? In three words - LACK OF SLEEP. The newborn stage can be difficult because you'll be feeding and caring for them around the clock, on their schedule. Newborns sleep about 14-17 hours a day, but this is in **fragments** rather than long segments.

Newborns have very short sleep and wake windows, meaning they sleep and wake in small segments - eat, sleep, poop, repeat.

Newborns also do not yet have a circadian rhythm established so they cannot distinguish day from night. They need to be fed throughout the night because their stomachs are very small, and therefore can only eat small, frequent volumes.

The numbers of hours your baby sleeps are not something you can control, nor can you put them onto a schedule. Throughout the day, try to keep naps in a noisy and well-lit area and do not let any one nap go longer than 2 hours. In the first month of life, the average time your baby is awake between naps is only 30 minutes to 1 hour (just long enough to eat and get a diaper change usually).

Remember, feeding and sleeping patterns will look different from day to day and should be all baby led – your baby is the boss! Sleep training and cry-it-out techniques can create unhealthy attachment. Babies naturally want to be near you, you are their whole habitat.

At night, remember babies are very active in REM sleep and can make noises and frequent movements. Try not to react to each small noise your baby makes because you are probably waking them from active sleep. They make look like they are awake, but they are actually asleep! If you are a light sleeper, try sleeping with an earplug in one ear to soften your reactions to your baby or try a sound machine or fan with fluctuating sounds rather than static/white noise.

I could write a whole book on newborn sleep cycles and wake windows, but why reinvent the wheel? For more information on sleep cycles and wake windows, visit the following link.

WHEN DO YOU GET TO SLEEP?

You can always follow the age-old saying of "sleep when the baby sleeps" throughout the day and night, but sometimes napping throughout the day can make you groggy and make you feel worse rather than better.

To combat this, try instead to just get in bed earlier – like 6pm early if you need to. Get ready for bed, get into bed, then sleep **in bed** when baby is sleeping at night. Then, sleep in late in the morning – like 11AM late if you need to!

Yes, this will make your days shorter, but they will slowly lengthen each day as your baby's sleep and awake segments get longer as they age!

At night, your infant's first stretch of sleep is generally the longest. It can be tempting to stay up to get some alone time when your baby first falls asleep but use this sleep time wisely. To get your baby to sleep, you can "top off" your baby after breastfeeding with a bottle of expressed breast milk from the night before. Breast milk expressed from the middle of the night naturally has higher amounts of sleep hormones such as melatonin and tryptophan. These hormones help your baby fall asleep and stay asleep, which is why supplementing with this milk at the last feed before bed can help.

SECOND NIGHT SYNDROME

Second night syndrome is a phenomenon that usually occurs about 24 hours after birth. Your baby will want to be on the breast constantly but will quickly fall asleep. Then, if put down, your baby will probably wake up and fuss to get back on the breast. If re-latched, your baby may feed for a short time and fall back asleep. You may go back and forth many times and it can be very frustrating. There is light at the end of the tunnel, this is just temporary, and the below strategies can help.

Hold your baby skin-to-skin. Skin-to-skin holding is very soothing for baby, and they feel secure attachment when they feel and smell their mothers' body.

Offer the breast when your baby wants to eat. Frequent nursing is the key to an abundant milk supply. This is called feeding on demand; you create a supply based on the demand of your baby.

Assure that baby is latching well at the breast. If your baby is not latching well, then they might not be getting the milk that is in the breast because they cannot properly empty it. Remember to look for the wide mouth (lots of double chins) and listen for swallows every 3-15 sucks. The latch should be deep and asymmetrical. Refer to the chapter on latching.

Nap between feeds, nap when the baby naps. Try to take a short cat nap each time your baby naps, especially at night. Take advantage of the time you have between feeds. It can help to swaddle your baby to your chest in kangaroo care with a responsible person watching to make sure you are safe.

Ask for help. Work out a plan with your partner or support person or anyone who can spend the night with you. They can take turns holding, walking, and rocking the baby between feeds so you can sleep.

Practice good sleep hygiene throughout the day and night. By creating patters of day and nighttime sleep, your baby will slowly start to differentiate day from night sleep and create sleep habits. THIS TAKES TIME. During the day, keep the environment bright and noisy. Then at night, keep the sleep space dark and use just enough dim light to make sure your latch is correct. Keep nighttime feeds "boring" and quiet. Keep in mind, your baby waking frequently at night does not mean you are doing anything wrong. Hormones for milk production are highest at night, so it is your baby's natural drive to want to cluster feed during this time to support and increase your milk supply.

Try the side-lying breastfeeding position. By bringing baby next to you in the "cuddle curl" position in bed, you can safely breastfeed. If you fall asleep while baby is breastfeeding, make sure you are practicing the safe sleep seven. Accidents happen when you are fighting sleep, are exhausted and babies are dropped or end up in unsafe sleeping positions.

Know you are not alone. All over the world there are other moms awake at 3AM rocking their babies back to sleep. This is just temporary.

Keep your baby awake for the entire feeding session. See the next chapter on waking a sleepy baby.

WAKING A SLEEPY BABY

Babies are often sleepy during the first few days and weeks of life, especially during the daytime hours. They may not wake often enough to feed 8-12 times in 24 hours. Or, once the feeding has begun, they may fall asleep at the breast and not successfully complete the feeding. It is important to keep your baby awake as long as possible **during** the feeding and fully awake **before** feeds. This will ensure a feed is successful and effectively emptying your breasts. Throughout the *daytime* hours, try to wake and feed your baby every 2 hours if they do not wake on their own to eat.

- Hold baby skin-to-skin for at least 15-30 minutes.
- Undress baby to a diaper
- Change positions or attempt to burp baby prior to feeding.
- Rub and massage baby's head, bottom of feet, up and down spine, across belly, up and down arms, etc.
- Do baby "sit-ups" by rocking baby from sitting to lying position and back again. Rock gently back and forth until baby's eyes open. Do not "jack-knife" the baby or force forwards.
- Talk to the baby.
- Change the baby's diaper.

- Apply cool washcloth to baby's head, stomach or back (do not let baby become chilled)
- Allow baby to suck on finger for a few minutes with drops of colostrum or breast milk.
- Express a few drops of colostrum or breast milk under your baby's nose, onto lips, or into baby's mouth.

During nighttime feeds after the first few weeks of life, consider doing feeds where baby is not fully awake for the feed. For example, when you feel your breasts are full and they wake you, pull your baby out of the bedside bassinet and latch them to your breast. They will need to be simulated enough to obtain a deep latch, but do not need to be fully awake. This technique can help prevent your baby from waking up hungry/hangry and instead you will fill their stomach before they wake on their own. By doing so, you will feed them back to sleep and prevent them from fully waking, extending their sleep time. After the feed, you both can go right back to sleep and avoid a full wake window.

LATCHING PROBLEMS + SORE OR DAMAGED NIPPLES

Always consult with a lactation consultant for latching difficulties. Sometimes, it's just a quick and easy fix. It is better to intervene sooner, before your nipples become too damaged, rather than later. Some people will tell you, "It's normal to have cracked or bleeding nipples, you just need to get used to it." Remember, nipple damage is NOT normal.

Nipple **soreness** can be normal, especially in the first few weeks, but nipple **damage** is not normal and is a sign that something needs to be corrected. Nipple soreness usually is the worst with the initial latch-on. This pain with latch-on should go away the first ~20 seconds of your breastfeeding session. If the pain does not go away, break the latch, and try again. However, if you have nipple damage such as cracked, bleeding, bruised, etc. nipples, then you should consult with a lactation consultant immediately.

Always contact your healthcare provider for concerns with infection or if you have flu-like symptoms or a fever.

Here is a video about preventing sore/damaged nipples and how to treat them:

Problem	Cause	Solution
Creased nipple after latch	-Shallow latch -Symmetrical latch -Tongue/lip ties -Positioning of baby	-Deeper latch -Check baby's oral anatomy to rule out a tongue tie/lip tie (see Pediatrician and Lactation Consultant) -Position baby with nose aimed at nipple -Asymmetrical latch -Wait for baby's mouth to be open >140 degrees before latching on
Sore or sensitive nipples	-Early breast-feeding -Nipple skin is stretching	-Deeper latch -Stretching is normal – apply lanolin/nipple cream/breast-milk to keep nipples hydrated -Asymmetrical latch -Utilize nipple shells to protect nipples between feeds -May use nipple shield as a tool to protect

		nipples during feeding (ensure proper latch FIRST before going to a nipple shield)
Pain at latch-on, goes away after a few seconds	-Stretching of nipple skin -Already damaged nipples, but deep latch	-Stretching is normal – apply lanolin/nipple cream/breast-milk to keep nipples hydrated -Ensure deep, asymmetrical latches -Utilize nipple shells to protect nipples between feeds
Painful/bruised nipples	-Shallow latch -Symmetrical latch -Positioning of baby -Tongue/lip ties	-Deeper latch -Massage to trigger letdown reflex -Check baby's oral anatomy to rule out a tongue tie/lip tie (see Pediatrician and Lactation Consultant) -Position baby with nose aimed at nipple -Asymmetrical latch

		-Use lanolin before/after feedings
Blister on the tip of nipple	-Shallow latch -Symmetrical latch -Tongue/lip ties	-Deeper latch -Check baby's oral anatomy to rule out a tongue tie/lip tie (see Pediatrician and Lactation Consultant) -Position baby with nose aimed at nipple -Asymmetrical latch -Use lanolin before/after feedings
Cracked/bleeding nipples	-From friction on roof of baby's mouth -Shallow latch -Symmetrical latch	-Deeper latch -Check baby's oral anatomy to rule out a tongue tie/lip tie (see Pediatrician and Lactation Consultant) -Position baby with nose aimed at nipple -Asymmetrical latch -Wait for baby's mouth to be open >140 degrees

		before latching on -Rinse skin with clean water, wash hands regularly, apply lanolin
Inflamed, red skin on nipple tip/areola	-Possible infection (bacterial, yeast, or both) -Possible contact dermatitis from cream/ointment -Shallow latch	-Rinse with water before and after feeds -Contact primary care OBGYN for diagnosis and treatment -Hand express/pump and cup/bottle/syringe feed if latch is too painful -Anti-inflammatory meds may help
Shooting pain radiating from nipple	-Pain follows the nerves in the breast/nipple -Trauma from biting/gumming -Possible infection	-Contact primary care OBGYN -Deeper latches -Check baby's oral anatomy to rule out a tongue tie/lip tie (see Pediatrician and Lactation Consultant)

Flat/dimpled/inverted nipple	Nipple anatomy	-May need to use a nipple shield -Pump for a few minutes to evert the nipples before latching -Use nipple everters (can start during pregnancy)
Engorgement	-Breasts fill with milk faster than they are emptied	-Hand express to soften the breasts to comfort -Express in a warm shower -Cold packs on the breasts after feeding, warmth prior to feeding -Do NOT pump until you are empty, try to breastfeed 8-12 times in 24 hours
Nipple slides in and out of baby's mouth	-Pre-term babies -Long nipples	-Pull baby in towards your breast while latched (you should not be able to see the nipple in the corner of your baby's mouth)

		-Pull baby on closer, support the shoulders/neck
Nipple tip is blanched (white) after feeds, or red/blue after feeds	-Vasospasm -Previous nipple injury -Poor blood flow to nipple -Shallow latch	-Keep nipple and breast warm -Deep, asymmetrical latch -Contact OBGYN - prescribed vasodilators may help
Hearing a clicking/smacking sound while latched	-Breaks in suction -No seal of lips -Symmetrical latch -Tongue/lip ties	-Check baby's oral anatomy to rule out a tongue tie/lip tie (see Pediatrician and Lactation Consultant) -Break the latch and try again -Asymmetrical latch -Chin support
Disorganized sucking pattern	-Pre-term baby -Fast delivery	-Suckle training
Cough/Choke	-High supply -Strong let-down reflex -Tongue/lip ties -Full stomach	-Check baby's oral anatomy to rule out a tongue tie/lip tie (see Pediatrician

		and Lactation Consultant) -1st 24 hours, full belly of amniotic fluid -Feed in a semi-reclined position to reduce let-down flow -Burp baby often and between breasts -Keep baby upright after feeding
Sleepy baby	-First 24 hours of life -Low supply	-Wake baby for feeds every 2-3 hours, at least 8 times in a 24-hour period -Pump/hand express and supplement with expressed breast milk via bottle, spoon, or syringe -Finger feeding to take baby -Get baby naked (except diaper) for feedings -Stimulate baby to stay awake while feeding

		(blow in face, tickle feet, etc.)
Over stimulated baby, crying at breast	-HANGRY baby -Pushing on back of head -Forcing baby onto breast	-Try feeding baby before they are hungry – follow the early signs of hunger -Wear baby skin-to-skin until they have calmed -Hand express/pump small amount and feed to baby as a "snack" to calm baby before latching -Gently support the neck/shoulder blades behind the ears rather than the back of baby's head
Tongue smacking	-May be hungry -Humped or bunched tongue	-Finger feeding - Suckle training
Baby pushes tongue onto nipple, pushes nipple out of mouth	-Tongue thrusting -Pre-term	-Suckle training -Allow baby to lick nipple first, allow open mouth >140

		degrees before latching
Receding jaw/chin	-Normal in newborns	-Position baby with nose aimed at nipple -Asymmetrical latch
Dimpled cheeks	-Shallow latch -Pre-term -Symmetrical latch	-Deeper latch -Check baby's oral anatomy to rule out a tongue tie/lip tie (see Pediatrician and Lactation Consultant) -Position baby with nose aimed at nipple -Asymmetrical latch -Wait for baby's mouth to be open >140 degrees before latching on

REMINDER: If you have nipple damage such as cracked, bleeding, bruised, etc. nipples, then you should consult with a lactation consultant immediately.

Always contact your healthcare provider for concerns with infection or if you have flu-like symptoms or a fever.

FORMULA AKA HUMAN MILK REPLACEMENT

It may not seem like offering your baby a bottle of infant formula has any consequences. However, it does. And there are risks to feeding just one bottle of infant formula. New research indicates even a small volume of formula causes sensitization to cow milk protein and alters the infant's gut biome, which can lead to cow milk protein allergies later in life.

It may be surprising there are risks of not breastfeeding. The longer the mother breastfeeds, the lower the risks.

Before you make a decision, consider these things. Ask your nurse, physician, or lactation consultant for more details if you have questions.

For baby, not breastfeeding causes increased risk of:
- ✓ Infections (lung and GI tract)
- ✓ Childhood obesity
- ✓ Type 1 and type 2 diabetes
- ✓ Childhood cancer
- ✓ Sudden infant death syndrome
- ✓ Otitis media (ear infections)
- ✓ Lower respiratory tract infections
- ✓ Asthma
- ✓ Atopic dermatitis (skin allergies)

✓ Heart disease and high blood pressure
✓ Diarrhea
✓ Necrotizing Enterocolitis in premature infants
✓ Colic and stomach upset
✓ Changes the digestive bacteria in your baby's GI tract
✓ Dental malocclusion

If you are breastfeeding, offering ONE bottle of formula can:
✓ Reduce your breast milk supply
✓ Change your baby's suck at the breast
✓ Sensitization to cow's milk protein, may lead to cow milk protein allergies
✓ Reduce your baby's desire to breastfeed

For mom, not breastfeeding causes increased risk of:
✓ Premenopausal breast cancer
✓ Ovarian cancer
✓ Obesity
✓ Retained pregnancy weight gain
✓ Type 2 diabetes
✓ Myocardial infarction (heart attack)
✓ Metabolic syndrome
✓ Osteoporosis
✓ Rheumatoid arthritis

DID YOU KNOW: If infants were breastfed optimally (6 months exclusively, continuing for a year or more), it would save 3,340 lives from only

3 diagnoses (breast cancer, hypertension, and MI) annually.

Also, if infants were breastfed optimally (6 months exclusively, continuing for a year or more), it would save 721 infant lives and $14 billion annually.

WHEN TO SUPPLEMENT WITH FORMULA:

If your pediatrician or lactation consultant recommends supplementing your baby with formula for a **medical** reason, just remember to use the BRAIN acronym and know the reason why they are recommending formula. Does the benefit of using formula outweigh the risks of not breastfeeding? Can you start pumping and triple feeding to supplement with breast milk rather than formula? Are they aware of the risks of not breastfeeding? Formula companies have created a "formula" to mimic breast milk, but have you read the ingredients?

There is a time and place where formula is required for medical reasons, but these circumstances are rare.

You may hear the phrase "fed is best" to combat the terrible mom shaming that comes along with formula feeding. I am here to say, please eliminate this phrase from your mind because it is setting you up for self-doubt and failure. You can do this; trust your body. Yes, it is of course better for your baby to be fed rather than not fed, but this phrase "fed is best" is fueled by formula companies pushing their agenda and making moms doubt their bodies. For breastfeeding to work, you cannot hyper fixate on amounts of breast milk you are feeding or how much volume your baby is getting. We are growing humans, not baking.

Remember, if you feed formula AKA human milk replacement you are in fact replacing your own human milk. Each time you supplement, you are essentially decreasing your milk supply by that volume because you are not emptying it from your breast. If your baby is full of formula, they are not breastfeeding or stimulating your breasts, which decreases your supply. This is known as a negative feedback loop.

If you feed formula and want to continue to breastfeed, it is important to protect your milk supply by stimulating and properly emptying the breasts each time you supplement with the formula. If you do not protect your supply by stimulating the breasts, then your supply will decrease as you tell your body, "My baby is not hungry because they did not need my milk, you can make less." This decrease of supply is a vicious cycle to get into when formula feeding, especially when moms don't understand this negative feedback loop.

To conclude, if your healthcare provider recommends formula as a supplement, be sure you are making an informed decision. There are valid medical reasons for supplementation, but they are rare. Before jumping to formula, demand to meet with an IBCLC lactation consultant to consider alternative feeding methods.

PUMPING

If you plan to exclusively breastfeed, chances are you will be separated from your baby at one time or another during your breastfeeding journey. For most moms, the separation begins when she returns to work. Separation from the baby is the most common reason for pumping with a breast pump, but not the only one.

If you plan to exclusively breastfeed, it is best to wait to pump until breastfeeding is well established (usually 3-4 weeks) to allow your supply to be based on your baby's demand at the breast. If you start pumping before then, it can negatively affect your supply by giving an *excessive* oversupply or even an undersupply. However, if you are separated from your baby for any reason, the pump can be used to mimic your baby's pattern of emptying your breasts. The breast pump basically "replaces" your baby at the breast.

Some moms prefer the use of a breast pump over breastfeeding directly at the breast because they have painful latching, babies refuse to latch, or even because of nipple damage. In these scenarios, it is best to seek professional assistance from an IBCLC to find out the cause of these problems.

Some moms make the choice to both pump and breastfeed, whereas others exclusively pump throughout their breastfeeding experience. Some moms pump because they feel it is easier to pump than to latch. In contrast, others dislike pumping for the same reason; they feel latching and breastfeeding at the breast is much easier than pumping.

When choosing a breast pump, it is a very personal decision because it is based on your *reason* for pumping. Some moms breastfeed exclusively at the breast and hate pumping because cleaning all the pump parts can be tedious. For these moms, a Haakaa or a manual breast pump is sufficient for the purpose of building a milk stash with excess milk volume while still exclusively breastfeeding at the breast. For women who plan to go back to work early, and their breast pump is meant to maintain their milk supply, a more robust pump such as a double electric breast pump may be the best choice. The same goes for women who are exclusively pumping; they should look for a double electric breast pump that has sufficient power, suction, and adjustment on settings. For these women, a rechargeable battery may be important if they will be on-the-go or without access to an electric outlet. Also, portability and bulk may be a factor in choosing a pump if you are going to be transporting it often.

Keep in mind, some women don't get a sufficient let-down (AKA milk ejection reflex) when pumping and the output from the pump is very minimal. This does not mean you do not have enough milk in your breasts, it just means a pump is not the best thing at emptying them out. Babies are the most efficient at emptying the breasts and most people do not respond to the breast pump as well as to their baby.

Overall, the choice of which pump to choose is a very personalized one which is why there isn't a one-size-fits-all solution for breast pumps. An experienced IBCLC can help you choose a breast pump that is best for your needs.

FLANGE SIZING

The flange is the part of the breast pump that fits over and around your nipple while you are pumping. If the flange is too big, your nipple and areola will be tugged into the tunnel of the flange and will cause nipple damage. However, if the flange is too small, the sides of the nipple will rub onto the sides of the flange and tunnel, causing blistering and nipple damage from the friction.

Having a correct flange fit while pumping is like having a correct latch while breastfeeding; if the flange fit is incorrect, the breasts will not be emptied efficiently or effectively.

To choose the correct flange size, it is best to have an experienced IBCLC measure and assess your nipples while pumping. Mothers can use the trial-and-error method or measure their own nipples but remember, using the wrong flange size can cause significant nipple damage. To measure your nipples, measure the diameter of the tip of the nipple. This measurement plus 3-4mm will generally be your flange size. It is important, however, to also assess the way the nipple moves in the flange while pumping and how it *feels*. If you are feeling pain while pumping, the flange probably needs to be adjusted, but it could also be many other components. This is why, if you are having any pain or minimal output while pumping, it's important to see an experienced IBCLC to problem solve and find a solution that works for your breasts and nipples.

Most breast pumps come with a standard 24mm flange size in their pumps, but a very small number of women actually fit a 24mm flange size. The majority of women will be much smaller than this, and some much larger. There are silicone flange inserts that fit into this 24mm flange size and come in various sizes. By purchasing these inserts, it allows you to try different sizes based on your comfort and even go up or down by millimeters. This flexibility in sizing is important as your nipples change size and shape throughout your breastfeeding journey. This is the method I most commonly recommend because it allows for slight adjustments to make you more comfortable and the pumping sessions more effective.

CLOGGED DUCTS AND MASTITIS

Mastitis is defined as a *spectrum* of conditions resulting from ductal inflammation and narrowing, rather than a just simple "clog." It is normally noticed when an area of the breast tissue is red, visibly inflamed, painful, and hot to the touch.

When people think of clogged ducts and mastitis, they think of them as going hand in hand. As in, a "clog" of milk sits for too long within the breast and that leads to mastitis. This can be the case, but more times than not, mastitis is due to the narrowing of the ducts due to congestion and inflammation. This congestion is generally due to hyperlactation (AKA breastmilk oversupply) or an imbalance in mom's bacteria or microbiome.

This is why having an oversupply of breastmilk (like you often see from pumping moms showing off on Instagram and TikTok) is not generally a good thing! Think of a milk oversupply like a traffic jam within the breast; where there are too many cars on the road it creates traffic. Just like when you have too much milk, it creates inflammation within the breast which compresses the ducts like a pinched hose, not allowing the breast to empty fully. This milk stasis is what leads to "clogged ducts" and if not treated, can lead to mastitis. This is why advice like "pump,

pump, pump!" and "massage, massage, massage!" are contradicted when you have signs and symptoms of a "clogged duct" because you are telling your body to put more cars on an already jammed road. Excessive pumping will just further exacerbate the problem as you're telling the body to make more milk. By excessively emptying the breasts, you're creating even more oversupply and more inflammation.

I like to think of a clogged duct and mastitis as an inflamed pimple. I know it might be a gross analogy to same, but bear with me. I think most of us have had a pimple that was teeny, and we turned it into a giant crater by picking, which is why this analogy is easy to understand. If you *gently* coax out the pus from a pimple, normally you can pop it easily. However, if you poke and prod, squeeze, and massage, it makes the area more inflamed. This inflammation in the skin surrounding the pimple compresses the pore (or duct) that you're trying to get the pus through, which makes it impossible to pop and makes the pimple much worse. This is very similar to the inflammation within your breast with mastitis. It is an inflammation of the breast tissue around the ducts that can be caused by many things, but the underlying issue is the milk not being able to be removed due to the ductal narrowing.

The other most common cause if mastitis is dysbiosis (or imbalance) in the breast microbiome due to things such as antibiotics, probiotics, overuse of breast pumps, and even use of nipple shields. This imbalance can happen when nipple shields and pumps don't allow the exchange of healthy bacteria between mom and baby. Also, when the whole body's microbiome is off such as with antibiotics or too many probiotics an imbalance in the microbiome of the breasts can result.

So, if you aren't supposed to "pump, pump, pump" or massage and squeeze to empty out the "clog," (because this will make it much WORSE) how do you reduce the inflammation within your breast?

The solution: Frequent, effective milk removal from the breast, without overstimulating by excessively pumping. What does this mean? Moms should continue breastfeeding on both breasts on demand and at least 8-12 times in 24 hours. They should not aim to "empty" the breasts. If pumping, moms should only express milk to comfort, not until empty, to avoid creating more oversupply. Overstimulation of the breasts can make the problem much worse because of supply and demand.

Additionally, the use of ice and anti-inflammatories such as ibuprofen can reduce the inflammatory response in the breast tissue. Also, OTC Tylenol can be effective at reducing pain.

Moms should also follow the other rules and recommendations of breastfeeding found in the Breastfeeding & Latching chapter of this book such as not going longer than 5 hours at night between feeds and obtaining a deep, asymmetrical latch to prevent milk stasis.

Many mastitis symptoms will resolve with conservative care, without antibiotics. Always follow your HCP's guidelines on when to seek medical care. For the scientific research regarding mastitis, visit the QR code shown to the right.

MEDICAL DISCLAIMER: The information provided in this book is intended solely for general educational and informational purposes only. It is neither intended nor implied to be a substitute for professional medical advice. Always seek the advice of your healthcare provider for any questions you may have regarding your or your infant's medical condition. Never disregard professional medical advice or delay in seeking it because of something you have received in this book.

JAUNDICE

Jaundice is the yellowing of your baby's skin due to a high buildup of bilirubin in their system. Bilirubin is a byproduct of the breakdown of red blood cells (RBC's) in your body by the liver and is eliminated from the body in poop. That's why your baby's poop in the first few days is black – from the RBC's (these first poops are called meconium). Jaundice can happen right after birth in newborns, especially if mom and baby have different blood types, specifically different RH factors. If you received Rhogam during pregnancy or are O+, then your baby's blood type will be checked after delivery. Some babies are at a higher risk for jaundice for other reasons; ask your nurse/pediatrician if this is the case for your baby.

Jaundice can also happen because of limited intake; if your baby is not getting enough to eat then they will not poop as much. Remember, Bilirubin is eliminated from the body in poop, so if your baby is not eating then they are not pooping. If your baby is not pooping then the bilirubin builds up in the body, leading to jaundice.

The way to reduce Jaundice in your baby is to feed more volume to increase you baby's output. Placing your baby in indirect sunlight can also help the body to break down the bilirubin. Sometimes, if the level of bilirubin gets too high, your pediatrician may recommend phototherapy, which is blue light therapy and helps the body break down the bilirubin similarly to the way indirect sunlight does. Here is a video explaining Jaundice:

UMBILICAL CORD AND BATHING

The umbilical cord stump should fall off in 1-2 weeks. It helps to think of it like a scab. Do not submerge in water until it falls off and do not put anything on it, it should dry out. If it looks infected (reddened around the base, leaking green/yellow pus) call the pediatrician immediately.

If the umbilical cord stump falls off too early, sometimes you may see some bleeding. Call your pediatrician if this happens as they can apply a chemical agent called Silver Nitrate to the stump or the wound base to stop the bleeding. Once the cord dries out completely, it will fall off leaving your baby's little belly button!

When bathing your newborn in the first few weeks (and even months) of life, you want to sponge bathe your baby, rather than submerge them in water. Swaddling them in a light blanket or muslin swaddle, then pouring warm water over them slowly and cleaning each body part individually is usually the least stressful way to bathe a baby and they are less likely to cry.

Baths can be a stressful event for babies, but this technique called a "swaddle bath," can minimize stress. Babies are not the best at regulating their temperature, which is why it's the safest and easiest to bathe using this technique.

In general, bath time with a newborn should only be 5-10 minutes long and remember to be mindful of their body temperature as they can quickly become overheated or too cold.

HOW TO SWADDLE BATHE:

1. When preparing your baby for bath time, loosely swaddle them in a baby swaddle, thin blanket, or sheet.
2. With your newborn baby loosely swaddled, pour water over their body to dampen the entire swaddle.
3. While holding baby securely, the swaddle is gently un-swaddled on each limb individually, washed, rinsed and then re-swaddled before exposing the next body part.

During the bath, remember to clean all the skin folds well and dry them thoroughly after the bath. Do not forget to clean out behind the ears, between fingers and toes, inside the ear (with a damp cloth only), and in armpits. When areas are left damp after the bath, they are susceptible to yeast and bacterial growth and can lead to rashes and irritation.

Here is a video demonstrating a swaddle bath:

DIAPERING TIPS

Place a clean diaper underneath the dirty diaper, just in case baby decides to poop or pee again while you are changing them. You may go through more diapers in the beginning, as you get used to changing them. If you are using a wipeable changing pad, you can forgo this step, but it can be very helpful for changing diapers on fabric surfaces.

When securing the new diaper to your baby, make sure to fold the top of the fresh diaper down (inwards towards baby) below the umbilical cord to prevent rubbing on the cord (until the cord falls off). Also, to prevent blowouts, fold the back of baby's diaper inwards (towards them) to catch the poop in a "pocket" before it can get up their back. Make sure the fluffy edges of the diaper are all turned out (looking fluffy) to prevent blowouts. If you notice a rusty orange/brick color in baby's diaper, this is probably urate crystals and is very common in breastfed babies (about 22%) and can be normal in the first few days of life.

For boys, make sure their penis is always pointing down in the diaper. Also, be sure to cover their penis with a washcloth/wipe BEFORE completely removing/opening the diaper because they may pee on you when the penis come in contact with cold air. You can try to open the diaper, apply a cold wipe or cold air, then close it again to let them pee one last time in the diaper and avoid getting peed on. It is very normal and common for the scrotum to be swollen or enlarged; this will decrease over the next few days.

For girls, always wipe from front to back to avoid wiping stool into the vaginal opening. If you wipe from back to front, it can cause urinary tract infections from stool and bacteria entering the urethra. It can be normal to see discharge (sometimes pink tinged) from the vagina because of all the hormones from mom. Her external genitalia may also be swollen or enlarged; this will decrease in the next few days. Contact your pediatrician if you are concerned. See my video on tips for how to change a diaper below.

POSTPARTUM DEPRESSION & BABY BLUES

In the first two weeks after delivery, it is normal to cry for no reason, have mood swings, or just feel sad. This is normal due to things like hormone shifts, changes in your body, changes in your roles, and lack of sleep. We call this period the "baby blues." After about two weeks, or if you have deep feelings of sadness, this can be classified as postpartum depression.

Self-care is very important to feel like yourself. I don't mean going to get your nails done and getting a massage, I mean showering, changing your clothes at least once per day, and going outside. You may laugh if you are reading this before having your baby, but if you take only a few things away from this book, make it this! If you have other things that make you feel good like getting massages and shopping, add these in one by one.

SET A DAILY GOAL TO:
1. Shower once per day
2. Change your clothes once per day (even if it's into a different pair of pj's)
3. Get outside

When you go outside, make it a daily walk to get your exercise, if you're feeling up to it. Or just sit out in the sunlight for a few minutes each day. **Allow people to help you around the house**. Asking for help and utilizing other people doesn't make you weak or mean that you can't do it all on your own. We know you can do it; let us help *you* take care of *you*, so you can focus on taking care of your baby.

Make sure you are open in discussing how you've been feeling with your partner or people you trust. Also, at the postpartum visits with your health care provider, make sure you are discussing your emotions and feelings in addition to the medical examinations, this is very important.

Support groups really help you to not feel alone, because you aren't. The postpartum period can feel very isolating, but there are mothers all over the world feeling the same way you are right now. Sometimes, just seeing others with their new baby or breastfeeding and chatting can be a world of reassurance. The leader of support groups will sometimes be a lactation consultant who can also answer questions and help you troubleshoot problems.

It can take a while to find your groove, even several weeks for you and your baby to get into a pattern of feeding and nap times. Go with the flow and learn your baby's natural rhythms. Schedules don't work until the baby is out of the newborn stage.

DISCLAIMER: This information in my book is not intended to diagnose or treat any medical or psychological condition. Please consult your healthcare provider (HCP) for individual advice regarding your own situation. If you are experiencing an emergency or have thoughts of harming yourself or your baby, please call 9-1-1 or go to your local emergency room.

SUMMARY: SURVIVAL IN THE FIRST TWO WEEKS

Breastfeed whenever your baby shows hunger cues:
It sounds like a lot, but your baby needs your milk, and your breasts need stimulation to bring in an abundant milk supply, Newborns needs to be fed around the clock, so they get AT LEAST 8+ feedings in each 24-hour period.

Wear your baby:
Keep your baby skin-to-skin and on you as much as possible during these first few weeks and even months. By doing so, you can better respond to their needs and learn their cues.

Wake your baby well before feedings:
A drowsy baby will not feed for long. Undress to diaper, change a diaper, change positions, talk to baby, burp them, etc. until their eyes are open, and they are alert. A good strategy is to wear baby skin-to-skin for at least 15-30 minutes before feeding.

Feed on demand
It is important to feed you baby "on demand" by watching your baby rather than watching the clock. Try to feed your baby based on early signs of hunger. This can be very often and that's completely normal. If your baby shows signs of

hunger, get them back on the breast despite when they last fed.

Keep your baby awake for the whole feeding:
If your baby drifts off to sleep, "bug" your baby to keep them awake. Rub or massage feet or back, use cool wash cloths, or try to hand express into their mouth while latched to keep them interested. Try burping and switching breasts back and forth. Look for vigorous sucking on each breast.

If your breasts get engorged, have your baby empty them by frequently feeding:
Engorgement is common as mature milk comes in around day 3-5. Draining the breasts and gentle massage during feedings can help. You may use a breast pump prior to or after feeding to soften the breasts, but do not pump until empty, that will increase the engorgement. You can also try to hand express in the shower to relieve pressure, apply moist heat prior to feedings, and apply ice after feedings.

Watch for diaper output and weight gain:
The best way to know your baby is "getting enough" in the first week is by monitoring diapers. Baby should have output correlating with days old. After the first two weeks of life, monitoring weight based on your baby's growth curve is the best indication of intake volumes.

If your nipples get sore:
Sore nipples can be normal, damaged nipples are never normal. Try to "sandwich" the breast to

compress it as small as possible and give baby a big bite with a wide mouth. Aim for an asymmetrical latch and remember the three rules of latching: nose-to-nipple, tummy-to-tummy, and baby-to-breast. Reach out to a lactation consultant if you have nipple damage.

When do you get to sleep?
The age-old advice: sleep when your baby sleeps. Newborns feed a lot at night and sleep more during the day so try to nap when your baby does to maximize your sleep. Alternatively, just try to go to bed EARLY and sleep in LATE to get the maximum hours of sleep at night when its dark outside between feeds. You can encourage baby to spend more time awake during the day by feeding and playing. Do not let your baby sleep >2 hours at a time during each daytime nap.

Set a daily goal for self-care:
Shower and change your clothes once per day as a minimum goal for each day. Everything else is just an extra, but make sure you are doing this each day.

GEMS FROM EXPERIENCED MOMS

Take a breastfeeding class before delivery:
Breastfeeding is natural, but it does not always come easy. Learning the basics can help and practicing before you deliver will make a world of difference. Spend a little time learning about what happens after delivery.

Start breastfeeding right in the delivery room:
Your baby will be interested in feeding within a minutes after birth. Keep baby skin-to-skin and enjoy the early feeding when they are most alert.

It's all about the latch:
How your baby holds your nipple and areola in their mouth is the key for comfortable, successful breastfeeding. Make sure the mouth is opened wide and baby has a full mouthful. If it hurts, get help ASAP.

Feed through the night at first:
No matter how tired you are, you need to feed around the clock in the beginning. This will establish a supply of milk based on what your baby needs and assures your baby will gain weight quickly.

You don't need to pump right away:
Your newborn baby is the best pump; Frequent feedings get breastfeeding off to the best start. If a

breast pump does not become necessary for a medical reason, try not to use an electric pump until about 4 weeks postpartum when breastfeeding is well established. You can however use a Haakaa as soon as your mature milk is in but be conscious of creating an excessive oversupply.

Don't wait too long to try a bottle:
Breastfeed exclusively for the first 4 weeks at least, that gets breastfeeding off to the best start. If you are planning to go back to work or will need to give bottles at any point, start around 4 weeks and offer weekly to keep up practice. It takes different skills for baby to drunk from a bottle vs from the breast. The best milk to use in a bottle is pumped breast milk.

Nurse lying down:
Recline or lie on your side while baby feeds. Use pillows to get yourself comfortable. You need rest too. Changing breastfeeding positions regularly also helps to be sure all the areas of the breast are emptied.

Use it or lose it:
The best way to make more milk is to feed the baby. An "empty" breast makes more milk. Don't skip breastfeeding sessions in the early days. Stimulating "empty" breasts is what tells your body to make more milk.

HOW CAN YOUR SUPPORT PERSON HELP

Most people think it is a great plan to begin pumping immediately after delivery so your support person can "help" with feedings throughout the night. You do not want to skip these night feedings though because leaving your breasts full (>5hours) will greatly reduce your supply.

The best way your support person can help is to do everything you normally do around the house for you. This includes but is not limited to laundry, cooking, cleaning, grocery shopping, caring for other children, feeding, and tending to animals, etc.

The main goal of the support person should be to take care of mom and the house so mom can take care of baby. Mom's only job in the immediate postpartum period should be caring for the baby and everyone else should take care of mom.

Support people can help mom as needed by changing the baby's diaper, holding the baby while mom showers, and giving encouragement. The environment should optimally support mom's bonding with baby.

WHEN TO CALL A LACTATION CONSULTANT

Call a lactation consultant ANYTIME you are unsure if breastfeeding is going well. Below are some examples of when you should reach out.

Call a lactation consultant for additional instruction and support if your baby:
- Is jaundiced
- Refuses to latch
- Is not gaining weight quickly (<1oz per day)
- Cries a lot and is fussy
- Feeds "all the time"
- Is premature or late preterm
- Spits up "a lot"

Call a lactation consultant for additional instruction and support if you:
- Are pregnant and plan to breastfeed
- Have inverted nipples
- Have painful or cracked nipples
- Are engorged
- Are ill or need to have surgery
- Have a "low" milk supply
- Are returning to work
- Experience mastitis or clogged ducts
- Experience stress around feedings
- Need assistance with your breast pump
- Are receiving conflicting advice or discouragement to breastfeed

TO THE READER

I wrote this book because I saw a huge disconnect in mothers who wanted to breastfeed and *planned* to breastfeed but did not learn the basics prior to having their baby. It is extremely difficult to learn anything when you are sleep deprived. You can imagine it would be especially difficult to learn how to breastfeed when sleep deprived, your hormones are shifting, you're exhausted, and there is a hungry/screaming baby in your arms trying to latch.

It is so important to learn how to breastfeed before you deliver. If you can feed your baby whenever they are hungry, then the rest will come naturally. I would argue breastfeeding fulfills all your baby's basic needs – comfort, warmth, food, attachment. Because of this, babies can focus on growth and development and are less stressed, cry less, and develop faster.

Breastfeeding does not have to be difficult. The postpartum period does not have to be stressful. Support groups help, but do not use them for medical advice as sometimes they can be the blind leading the blind.

Always seek professional assistance from an experienced IBCLC when having difficulty latching or feeding your baby.

"Anytime you're [frustrated], just close your eyes and imagine you are 80 years old, and you have a time machine that is bringing you right back to this moment. And this is the only moment you will get with them again when they're young." -Peter Attia

Happiness is not circumstantial. It's your attitude and what you're going to decide to do with it. And the only currency that we have is gratitude. And if you don't have gratitude in your life, you better figure out how to get it… because this is as good as it gets." - Nathan Donnelly

If you tucked a healthy child into a warm bed, in a safe home last night, and woke up to their smiling face this morning, you have won the lottery of life." - The Motherhood Home

"The best part of being a mom is when your baby looks up at you and just smiles and stares because they know you are their person. They look up at you like nobody else is as important as you. And you know you have them like nobody else ever will." - Unknown

"I know it can be hard to get up every day and have these little people rely on you. I know it's hard to feel like sometimes your world is so small. I want to remind you; you are the world. You are the world those little ones revolve around. You are their nurture, their home, their comfort. You are everything to them. I hope on your hard days, you know how special you are." – Anonymous

The Postpartum Nurse
Miranda Farmer RN, BSN, CBS, IBCLC

Thank you for purchasing my book, I hope it was helpful for you! Congratulations on your growing family!

MEDICAL DISCLAIMER: The information provided is intended solely for general educational and informational purposes only. It is neither intended nor implied to be a substitute for professional medical advice. Always seek the advice of your healthcare provider for any questions you may have regarding your or your infant's medical condition. Never disregard professional medical advice or delay in seeking it because of something you have received in this information.

For additional online resources or to obtain a lactation consultation, please visit my website for more information.

WWW.THEPOSTPARTUMNURSE.ORG

REFERENCES

Centers for Disease Control and Prevention. (2020). Proper Storage and Preparation of Breast Milk. Retrieved from Centers for Disease Control and Prevention website: https://www.cdc.gov/breastfeeding/recommendations/handling_breastmilk.htm

Dekker, Rebecca. "Evidence on Erythromycin Eye Ointment for Newborns." *Evidence Based Birth®*, 4 Aug. 2017, evidencebasedbirth.com/is-erythromycin-eye-ointment-always-necessary-for-newborns/.

Dekker, Rebecca, and Anna Bertone. "Evidence On: The Vitamin K Shot in Newborns." *Evidence Based Birth®*, 9 Apr. 2019, evidencebasedbirth.com/evidence-for-the-vitamin-k-shot-in-newborns/.

Guideline: Delayed Umbilical Cord Clamping for Improved Maternal and Infant Health and Nutrition Outcomes. Geneva: World Health Organization; 2014. Background. Available from: https://www.ncbi.nlm.nih.gov/books/NBK310514/

Healthy Birth Your Way. (2009). Lamaze International, InJoy Birth & Parenting Education. Retrieved from https://www.lamaze.org/portals/0/docs/educators/healthybirth_booklet.pdf

Newborn Screening Program. (n.d.). Retrieved from www.cdph.ca.gov website: https://www.cdph.ca.gov/Programs/CFH/DGDS/Pages/nbs/default.aspx

Remien K, Majmundar SH. Physiology, Fetal Circulation. [Updated 2023 Apr 26]. In: StatPearls [Internet]. Treasure Island (FL): StatPearls Publishing; 2023 Jan-. Available from: https://www.ncbi.nlm.nih.gov/books/NBK539710/

The Safe Sleep Seven. (2018, November 28). Retrieved from La Leche League International website: https://www.llli.org/the-safe-sleep-seven/

(2023). Retrieved November 27, 2023, from Aap.org website: https://publications.aap.org/pediatrics/article/150/1/e2022057990/188304/Slee

TIKTOK VIDEO LINKS

https://www.tiktok.com/@thepostpartumnurse/video/7166326431545380138?is_from_webapp=1&sender_device=pc&web_id=7250575749239834155

https://www.tiktok.com/@thepostpartumnurse/video/7166319630078840106?is_from_webapp=1&sender_device=pc&web_id=7246862754032027182

https://www.tiktok.com/@thepostpartumnurse/video/7120646062779682094?is_from_webapp=1&sender_device=pc&web_id=7246862754032027182

https://www.tiktok.com/@thepostpartumnurse/video/7090152349234253098?is_from_webapp=1&sender_device=pc&web_id=7116644242446108206

https://www.tiktok.com/@thepostpartumnurse/video/7119608673625787690?is_from_webapp=1&sender_device=pc&web_id=7116644242446108206

https://www.tiktok.com/@thepostpartumnurse/video/7128171920570191146?is_from_webapp=1&sender_device=pc&web_id=7246862754032027182

https://www.tiktok.com/@thepostpartumnurse/video/7105512596488391979?is

_from_webapp=1&sender_device=pc&web_id=7246862754032027182

https://www.tiktok.com/@thepostpartumnurse/video/7171954619558415659?is_from_webapp=1&sender_device=pc&web_id=7246862754032027182

VISIT TIKTOK @THEPOSTPARTUMNURSE TO SEE ALL FREE EDUCATIONAL VIDEOS

ThePostpartumNurse

www.ThePostpartumNurse.org

Copyright © 2023 Miranda Farmer

Printed in Great Britain
by Amazon